بسم الله الرحمن الرحيم

# ISLAMIC THEOLOGY

## (‘ILM AL-KALĀM )

# ISLAMIC THEOLOGY

('ILM AL-KALĀM )

Murtaḍā Muṭahharī

Translated by

Ali Quli Qara'i

A catalogue record for this book is available from the British Library and the Australian National Library

**Ordering Information:**
Quantity sales. Special discounts are available on quantity purchases by corporations, associations, and others. For details, contact the distributor at the address below.

Shia Books Australia
www.shiabooks.com.au
info@shiabooks.com.au

ISBN 978-1-922583-18-5

**This English edition first published in 2016**
**Second Edition 2021**

**Cover picture by @mnshots**

# Contents

*Transliteration* ........ VII
*Publisher's Note* ........ IX
*Biography of the Author* ........ XI
Preface ........ 1
The Beginnings of *Kalām* ........ 3
Inquiry or Imitation? ........ 4
The First Problem ........ 5
*Al-Kalām al-'Aqlī and al-Kalām al-Naqlī* ........ 7
Definition and Subject Matter of *'Ilm Al-Kalām* ........ 8
The Term *'Ilm al-Kalām* ........ 9
The Various Schools of *Kalām* ........ 10
Mu'tazilites ........ 15
The Doctrine of *al-Tawḥīd* ........ 18
The Doctrine of Divine Justice ........ 21
Whatever Khusrow does is Sweet *(Shīrīn).* ........ 22
Retribution *(al-wa'd wa al-wa'īd)* ........ 24
*Manzilah Bayna al-Manzilatayn* ........ 25
*Al-Amr bi al-Ma'rūf wa al-Nahy 'an al-Munkar* ........ 27
Other Mu'tazilite Notions and Beliefs ........ 28
Theology ........ 29
Physics ........ 30
Human Problems ........ 30
Political and Social Problems ........ 31

Transitions in the History of the Mu'tazilites....................32
Ash'arites....................38
The *Shī'ite Kalām*....................46
The *Shī'ī* Standpoint....................53
(i) *Tawḥīd*....................56
(ii) *'Adl*....................58
(iii) Free Will and Freedom....................58
(iv) Inherent Morality or Immorality of Deeds....................59
(v) Grace (*Luṭf*) and Choice of the Best *(Intikhāb al-Aṣlaḥ)*.....60
(vi) Independence and Validity of Reason....................60
(vii) 'Aim' and 'Purpose' of Divine Acts....................61
(viii) Vision *(Ru'yah)* of God....................62
(ix) The Faith or Infidelity of the *Fāsiq*....................63
(x) The Infallibility *('Iṣmah)* of the Prophets and the Imāms....63
(xi) Forgiveness (*Maghfirah*) and Intercession (*Shafā'ah*).....63
Notes....................65
Index....................73

# Transliteration

| Symbol | Transliteration | Symbol | Transliteration |
|---|---|---|---|
| ء | ’ | أ | a |
| ب | b | ت | t |
| ث | th | ج | j |
| ح | ḥ | خ | kh |
| د | d | ذ | dh |
| ر | r | ز | z |
| س | s | ش | sh |
| ص | ṣ | ض | ḍ |
| ط | ṭ | ظ | ẓ |
| ع | ‘ | غ | gh |
| ف | f | ق | q |
| ک | k | ل | l |
| م | m | ن | n |
| ه | h | و | w |
| ی | y | ة | ah |
| Long Vowels | | Short Vowels | |
| آ | a | ـَ | a |
| ای | ī | ـِ | i |
| او | ū | ـُ | u |
| Persian Letters | | | |
| Symbol | Transliteration | Symbol | Transliteration |
| پ | p | چ | ch |
| ژ | zh | گ | g |

*At the end of Farsi words, 'eh', '-e', and '-ye' have been used.*

## Publisher's Note

This book is originally written by the great Muslim thinker and reformer Āyatullāh Murtaḍā Muṭahharī on Mysticism for B.A. students at the faculty of theology of the University of Tehran. The original book was published after Muṭahharī's martyrdom, and its English translation was first published by Islamic College for Advanced Studies (ICAS) in London and then in Malaysia in a collection entitled Understanding Islamic Sciences.

In the present edition, however, the biography of the author, transliteration of expressions as well as Farsi and Arabic names, bibliography, and index are added and incomplete references are completed.

This book deals with such topics as a brief history of ʻilm al-kalām and its various schools(Shīʻites, Muʻtazilites and Ashʻarites) , the doctrines of *tawḥīd*, divine justice, retribution , free will and Freedom, independence and validity of reason, vision of God, the infallibility of the prophets and the Imāms, intercession and so on.

We hope that this book would be an invaluable contribution to the Islamic thought and of great benefit for all readers in general and people of researcher in particular.

**Al-Mustafa International Research Institute (M.I.R.I.)**

## Biography of the Author

Murtaḍā Muṭahharī was born in a village some forty kilometres from Mashhad in 1338/1919–20. He received his earliest education mostly at the hands of his father and while still a child entered the Ḥawza 'Ilmiyya, the traditional educational establishment, of Mashhad, but soon afterwards left for Qum, the centre for religious education in Iran. While he was pursuing elementary studies there he was greatly affected by the lessons in *akhlāq* (Islamic ethics) given by Āyatullāh Imām Khumaynī, which Muṭahharī himself described as being, in reality, lessons in *ma'ārif wa sayr-u-sulūk* (the theoretical and practical approaches to mysticism). He later studied metaphysics (*falsafa*) with him, as well as jurisprudence (*uṣūl al-fiqh*). He was especially attracted by *falsafa*, theoretical mysticism (*'irfān*) and theology (*Kalām*), known as 'intellectual knowledge', and he went on to study these subjects with 'Allāmah Ṭabāṭabā'ī. His teachers in law (*fiqh*) were all important figures of the time, especially Āyatullāh Burūjirdī, who became the authoritative jurisconsult (*marja'-e taqlīd*), as well as head of the Ḥawza ʻIlmiyya of Qum, in 1945. Murtaḍā Muṭahharī studied both *fiqh* and *uṣūl al-fiqh* in the classes of Āyatullāh Burūjirdī for ten years. He was also deeply affected at about this time by lessons on *Nahj al-Balāghah* given by Mīrzā ʻAlī Āqā Shīrāzī Iṣfahānī, whom he had met in Isfahan. He later said that, although he had been reading this work since his childhood, he now felt that he had discovered a 'new world'. Subsequently, Muṭahharī became a well-known teacher in Qum, first in Arabic language and literature, and later in logic (*manṭiq*), *uṣūl al-fiqh*, *falsafa* and mysticism.

In 1952 Murtaḍā Muṭahharī moved to Tehran, where, two years later, he began teaching in the Theology Faculty of the University. Not only did he make a strong impression on students, but his move to Tehran also meant that he could become involved with organizations for political and social change. These Islamic associations were groups of students, engineers, doctors, merchants, etc., set up during the 1950s and 1960s; they formed the nucleus of the movement that was eventually to become the revolution. He was also a founder member of the Ḥusayniyya Irshād, which played a central role in the religious life of the capital during the four years of its existence until its closure by the authorities in 1973. At the same time he maintained his contact with traditional religious activities, teaching first in the Madrasa Marwī in Tehran and later back in Qum, and also preaching in mosques in Tehran and elsewhere in the country. Through his lectures, articles and books he became a famous and much-respected figure throughout Iran, but it was mainly among the students and teachers of the schools and universities that he was most influential, setting an example and inspiring them as a committed and socially aware Muslim with a traditional education who could make an intellectually appropriate and exciting response to modern secularizing tendencies.

His wide-ranging knowledge and scholarship are reflected in the scope of his writings, which cover the fields of law, philosophy, theology, history and literature. He was also one of the few high-ranking *'ulamā'* to be in continuous contact with Imām Khumaynī during the fifteen or so years in which the movement that led to the revolution was developing. He was actively engaged in all the stages of this movement. His life came to an abrupt and untimely end when he was shot in the street by an assassin after a meeting of the Revolutionary Council on the evening of 1 May 1979. Many mourners accompanied his funeral cortege from Tehran to Qum, where he was buried near the shrine of the sister of the eighth *Shī'ī* Imām. Shahīd Muṭahharī contributed a great deal to Islamic scholarship through his many publications, most of which have been translated into English. They include: *Training and Education in Islam*(Amin Research and Cultural Centre,Kuala Lumpur,2011), *The theory of knowledge: An Islamic Perspective*(Amin Research and Cultural Centre,Kuala Lumpur,2011),*Islamic Modest Dress* (Macmillan Publishing Company, Inc., 1990); *Universal*

*Prototype*, translated by Laleh Bakhtiar (Abjad Book Designers & Builders, 1989); *Ḥijāb*, translated by Laleh Bakhtiar (Abjad Book Designers & Builders, 1993); *Iqbāl* (Abjad Book Designers & Builders, 1993); *Reviving Islamic Ethos*; *Master and Mastership*; *Jurisprudence and Its Principles*; *Spiritual Discourses*; *The Awaited Saviour*; *Light within Me*; *The Goal of Life*; Man and Universe; *Polarization Around the Character of 'Alī Ibn Abī Ṭālib*; *Woman and Her Rights*; and *Anecdotes of Pious Men.*

Apart from the above-mentioned books, there are many other published works in Arabic and Persian.

## Preface

*'Ilm al-kalām* is one of the Islamic sciences. It treats of the fundamental Islamic beliefs and doctrines in which it is necessary for a Muslim to believe. It explains them, argues about them and defends them.

The scholars of Islam divide Islamic teachings into three parts:

1. Doctrines (*'aqā'id*): These constitute the issues that must be understood and believed in, such as the Unity of God, the Divine Attributes, universal and restricted prophethood, etc. However, there are certain differences between Muslim sects as to what constitutes the basic articles of faith (*uṣūl al-Dīn*) in which belief is necessary.

2. Morals (*akhlāq*): These consist of the commands and teachings relating to the spiritual and moral characteristics of human beings, such as justice, fear of God (*taqwā*), courage, chastity, wisdom, endurance, loyalty, truthfulness, trustworthiness, etc., and prescribe 'how' a human being should be.

3. The Law (*aḥkām*): Under this heading are discussed

the issues relating to practice and the correct manner of performing acts, such as, prayers (*ṣalāt*), fasting (*ṣawm*), *ḥajj*, *jihād*, *al-amr bil ma'ruf wa al-nahy 'an al-munkar*, buying, renting, marriage, divorce and division of inheritance.

The science that deals with the first of the above-mentioned is *'ilm al-kalām*. The study of the second is *'ilm al-akhlāq* (ethics). The study of the third is called *'ilm al-fiqh* (the science of jurisprudence). What is subjected to division in this classification is the corpus of Islamic teachings; that is, those things that constitute the content of Islam. It does not include all those Islamic studies that form the preliminaries for the study of Islamic teachings, such as literature, logic and occasionally philosophy.

In this classification the criterion behind division is the relationship of Islamic teachings to the human being: things that relate to human reason and intellect are called *'aqā'id*; things that relate to human qualities are called *akhlāq*; and things that relate to human action and practice are included in *fiqh*.

Although *fiqh* is a single discipline from the viewpoint of its subject, it consists of numerous disciplines from other viewpoints.

In any case, *'ilm al-kalām* is the study of Islamic doctrines and beliefs. In the past, it was also called *uṣūl al-Dīn* or *'ilm al-tawḥīd wa al-ṣifāt*.

## The Beginnings of *Kalām*

Although nothing definite can be said about the beginnings of *'ilm al-kalām* among Muslims, what is certain is that discussion of some of the problems of *kalām*, such as the issue of predestination (*jabr*) and free will (*ikhtiyār*) and that of Divine Justice, became current among Muslims during the first half of the second century of Hijrah. Perhaps the first formal centre of such discussions was the circle of al-Ḥasan al-Baṣrī (d. 110/728–29). Among the Muslim personalities of the latter half of the first century, the names of Ma'bad al-Juhanī (d. 80/699) and Ghaylān ibn Muslim al-Dimashqī (d. 105/723) have been mentioned, adamant defenders of the ideas of free will (*ikhtiyār*) and human freedom. There were others who opposed them and supported predestination (*jabr*). The believers in free will were called *qadariyyah* and their opponents were known as *Jabriyyah*.

Gradually the points of difference between the two groups extended to a series of other issues in theology, physics, sociology and other problems relating to man and the Resurrection, of which the problem of *jabr* and *ikhtiyār* was only one. During this period, the *qadariyyah* came to be called *Mu'tazilites* and the *Jabriyyah* became known as *Ash'arites*. The Orientalists and their followers insist on considering the beginnings of discursive discussions in the Islamic world from this point or thereabouts.

However, the truth is that rational argumentation about Islamic doctrines starts with the Holy *Qur'an* itself, and has been followed up in the utterances of the Holy Prophet (S) and especially in the sermons of Amīr al-Mu'minīn 'Alī (A.S.) – despite the fact that their style and approach are different from those of the Muslim *mutakallimīn*.[1]

## Inquiry or Imitation?

The Holy *Qur'an* has laid the foundation of faith and belief on thought and reasoning. Throughout, the *Qur'an* insists that men should attain faith through the agency of thought. In the view of the *Qur'an*, intellectual servitude is not sufficient for believing and understanding its basic doctrines. Accordingly, one should take up a rational inquiry of the basic principles and doctrines of the faith. For example, the belief that God is One should be arrived at rationally. The same is true of the prophethood of Muḥammad (S). This requirement resulted in the establishment of *'ilm al-'uṣūl* during the first century.

Many factors gave rise to the unprecedented realization among Muslims of the need to study the fundamentals of the Islamic faith and to undertake the task of defending them, a realization that led to the emergence of prominent *mutakallimīn* during the second, third and fourth centuries. These were: the embracing of Islam by various nations who brought with them a series of (alien) ideas and notions; the mixing and coexistence of the Muslims with peoples of various religions, such as Jews, Christians, Magians and Sabaeans, and the ensuing religious debates and disputes between the Muslims and those peoples; the emergence in the Islamic world of the *Zanādiqah*[2] – who were totally against religion – as a result of general freedom during the rule of the ʻAbbāsid Caliphs (as long as it did not interfere in matters of state politics); and the birth of philosophy in the Muslim world – which itself gave birth to doubts and scepticism.

## The First Problem

Apparently, the first problem that was discussed and debated by the Muslims was that of predestination and free will. This was natural, since it is a primary problem that is linked with human destiny and attracts the interest of every thinking adult. It is arguably impossible to find a society that has reached intellectual maturity in which this problem has not been raised. Moreover, the Holy *Qur'an* has a large number of verses on this subject, which inevitably instigate thought about it.[3]

Accordingly, there is no reason to try to seek another source for the origin of this problem in the Islamic world.

Orientalists, in order to negate the originality of Islamic

teachings, habitually try at any cost to trace the roots of all sciences that originated among Muslims to the world outside the domains of Islam, in particular the Christian world. They insist that the roots of *‘ilm al-kalām* should be acknowledged to lie outside Islam, and they make similar attempts and claims with regard to the study of grammar, prosody (and perhaps semantics, rhetoric and studies of literary and poetic devices) and Islamic *‘irfān.*

The problem of determinism and free will (*jabr wa ikhtiyār*) is the same as the problem of predestination and Divine Providence (*qaḍā’ wa qadar*); the first formulation relates to man and his free will, while the second one relates to God. This problem also raises the issue of Divine Justice, because there is an explicit connection between determinism and injustice, on the one hand, and free will and justice, on the other.

The problem of justice raises the issue of the essential good and evil of actions, and the latter in its turn brings in its train the problem of the validity of reason and purely rational judgements. These problems together lead to the discussion of Divine Wisdom (that is the notion that there is a judicious purpose and aim behind Divine Acts),[4] and thereby, gradually, to the debate about the unity of Divine Acts and the unity of the Attributes, as we shall explain later.

The formation of opposite camps in the debates of *kalām* later acquired a great scope and extended to many philosophical problems, such as substance and accident, nature of indivisible particles that constitute physical bodies, the problem of space, etc. This was because, in the view of the *mutakallimīn*, discussion of such issues was considered a prelude to the debate about theological matters, particularly those related to *mabda'* (primeval origin) and *ma'ād* (resurrection). In this way many of the problems of philosophy entered *'ilm al-kalām*, and now there are many problems common to both.

If one were to study the books on *kalām*, especially those written after the 7th/13th century, one would see that most of them deal with the same problems as those discussed by philosophers–especially Muslim philosophers–in their books.

Islamic philosophy and *kalām* have greatly influenced each other. One of the results was that *kalām* raised new problems for philosophy, and philosophy helped to widen the scope of *kalām*, in the sense that dealing with many philosophical problems came to be considered necessary in *kalām*. With God's help, we hope to give an example of each of these two results of reciprocal influence between philosophy and *kalām*.

## *Al-Kalām al-'Aqlī and al-Kalām al-Naqlī*

Although *'ilm al-kalām* is a rational and discursive discipline, it consists of two parts in terms of the preliminaries and fundamentals it uses in arguments:

1. *'Aqlī* (rational);
2. *Naqlī* (transmitted, traditional).

The *'aqlī* part of *kalām* consists of the material that is purely rational, and if there is any reference to n*aqlī* (tradition), it is for the sake of illumination and confirmation of a rational judgement. But in problems such as those related to Divine Unity, prophethood and some issues of Resurrection, reference to *naql* - the Book and the Prophet's Sunnah - is not sufficient; the argument must be purely rational.

The *naqlī* part of *kalām* consists of issues related to the doctrines of the faith - and it is necessary to believe in them - but since these issues are subordinate to the issue of prophethood, it is enough to quote evidence from the Divine Revelation or the definite *aḥādīth* of the Prophet (S), e.g. in issues linked with *imāmah* (of course, in the *shīʿī* faith belief in *imāmah* is considered a part of *uṣūl al-Dīn*) and most of the issues related with the Resurrection.

## Definition and Subject Matter of *'Ilm Al-kalām*

For a definition of *'ilm al-kalām*, it is sufficient to say that, 'It is a science that studies the basic doctrines of the Islamic faith (*uṣūl al-Dīn*). It identifies the basic doctrines, seeks to prove their validity and answers any doubts that may be cast upon them.'

In texts on logic and philosophy it is mentioned that every science has a special subject of its own, and that the various sciences are distinguished from one another by virtue of their separate subject matter. This is certainly true, and those sciences whose subject matter has a real unity are such. However, there is nothing wrong with forming a discipline whose unity of subject matter and the problems covered by it are arbitrary and conventional, in the sense that it covers diverse, mutually exclusive subjects, which are given an arbitrary unity because they serve a single purpose and objective. In sciences whose subject has an essential unity, there is no possibility of overlapping of problems. But in sciences in which there is a conventional unity among the issues, there is no reason why issues should not overlap. The commonness of the problems between philosophy and *kalām*, psychology and *kalām* or sociology and *kalām* is a result of this.

Some Islamic scholars have sought to define and outline the subject matter of *'ilm al-kalām*, and have expressed various opinions. But this is a mistake, because a clear-cut delineation of the subject of study is possible for only those sciences that have an essential unity among the problems dealt with. But in those sciences in which there is a conventional unity of problems dealt with, there can be no unity of subject. This issue cannot be discussed further here.

## The Term *'Ilm al-Kalām*

Why has this discipline been called *'ilm al-kalām* and when was this name given to it? Some have said that it was called *kalām* (literally, 'speech') because it gives an added power of speech and argument to one who is well versed in it. Some say that the reason lies in the fact that experts in this science habitually began their own statements in their books with the expression *al-kalām fī kadhā*. Others explain that it was called *kalām* because it discussed issues regarding which the Ahl al-Ḥadīth preferred to maintain complete silence. Yet according to others this name came to prominence when the issue as to whether the Holy *Qur'an* (called *kalāmun ilāhī*, the Divine Utterance)[5] is created (*makhlūq*) or not became a matter for hot debate among Muslims – a controversy that led to animosity between the two opposite camps and to much bloodshed. This is also the reason why that period is remembered as a 'time of severe hardship' – *miḥnah*. That is, since most of the debates about the doctrines of the faith revolved around the *ḥudūth* (createdness, temporality) or the *qidam* (pre-eternity) of the 'Utterance' or *kalām* of God, the discipline that discussed the principal doctrines of the faith came to be called *'ilm al-kalām* (literally, 'the science of the Utterance'). These are the various theories about the origin of the name *'ilm al-kalām*.

## The Various Schools of *Kalām*

Muslims differed with one another in matters of the Law (*fiqh*), following differing paths and dividing into various sects, such as Ja'farī, Zaydī, Ḥanafī, Shāfi'ī, Mālikī and Ḥanbalī, each of which has a *fiqh* of its own. Similarly, from the point of view of doctrine, they divided into various schools, each with its own set of principal doctrines. The most important of these schools are the Shī'ites, the Mu'tazilites, the Ash'arites and the Murji'ah.

Some may regret the division of Muslims into sects in

matters dealing with *kalām* and *fiqh* and wonder why they could not maintain their unity in these spheres. The difference in matters of *kalām* causes disunity in their Islamic outlook, and the disagreement in the matter of *fiqh* deprives them of the unity of action.

Both the question and the regret are justified. But it is important to note the two following points:

The disagreement in issues of *fiqh* among Muslims is not so great as to shatter the foundations of their unity of doctrinal outlook and mode of practice, which have so much in common that the points of difference are not capable of inflicting any serious damage.

1. Theoretical differences and divergences of views are inevitable in societies in spite of their unity and agreement in principles; and as long as the roots of the differences lie in methods of inference, and not in vested interests, they are even beneficial; because they cause mobility, dynamism, discussion, curiosity and progress. Only when the differences are accompanied by prejudices and emotional and illogical alignments and lead individuals to slander, defame and treat one another with contempt, instead of motivating them to endeavour to reforming themselves, that they are a cause of misfortune.

2. In the *shīʿī* faith, the people are obliged to imitate a living *mujtahid*, and the *mujtahidūn* are obliged to ponder the issues and form their opinions independently and not to be content with what has been handed down by the ancestors. *Ijtihād* and independence of thought

inherently lead to difference of views; but this divergence of opinions has given life and dynamism to the *shīʿī fiqh.* Therefore, difference in itself cannot be condemned. What is to be condemned is difference that originates in evil intentions and selfish interests, or difference on issues that drive Muslims on separate paths, such as the issue of *imāmah* and leadership; not difference in secondary and non-basic matters.

To examine the intellectual history of the Muslims in an attempt to find which differences originated in evil intentions, vested interests and prejudices, and which were a natural product of their intellectual life, whether all points of difference in the sphere of *kalām* should be regarded as fundamental, or whether all problems in *fiqh* should be regarded as secondary, or if it is possible that a difference in *kalām* may not be of fundamental significance whereas one in *fiqh* may have such importance – these are questions that lie outside the brief scope of this discussion.

Before we turn to the schools of *kalām*, it is essential to point out that there has been a group of scholars in the Islamic world who were basically opposed to the very idea of *ʿilm al-kalām* and rational debate about Islamic doctrines, considering it a taboo and an innovation in the faith (*bidʿah*). They are known as Ahl al-Ḥadīth. Aḥmad ibn Ḥanbal, one of the imams of jurisprudence of the Ahl al-Sunnah, stands foremost among them.

The Ḥanbalīs are totally against *kalām*, Muʿtazilites or Ashʿarite, not to speak of the *shīʿī kalām.* In fact, they are basically opposed to logic and philosophy. Ibn Taymiyyah, who was one of the eminent scholars of the *Sunnī* world, gave a verdict declaring *kalām* and logic 'unlawful'. Jalāl al-Dīn al-Suyūṭī, another figure among the Ahl al-Ḥadīth, has written a book called *Ṣawn al-Manṭiq wa al-Kalām 'an al-Manṭiq wa al-Kalām* ('Protecting Speech and Logic from [the Evil of] *'ilm al-kalām* and the Science of Logic').

Mālik ibn Anas is another *Sunnī* Imām who considers any debate or inquiry about doctrinal matters to be unlawful. I have explained the *Shī'ī* viewpoint in this matter in the introduction to Vol. V of *Uṣūl-e Falsafah wa Rawishe Ri'ālism*.[6]

The important schools of *kalām*, as mentioned earlier, are *Shī'ī*, Mu'tazilah, Ash'arite and Murji'ah. Some sects of the Khawārij and the Bāṭinīs, such as the Ismā'īlīs, have also been considered as schools of Islamic *kalām*.[7]

However, in my view, none of these two sects can be considered as belonging to the schools of Islamic *kalām*. The Khawārij held specific beliefs in matters of doctrine and perhaps were the first to raise doctrinal problems by expressing certain beliefs about *imāmah*, the *kufr* (apostasy) of the *fāsiq* (evil-doer, one who commits major sins) and considered the disbelievers in these beliefs to be apostates. But, first, they did not create a rationalist school of thought in the Muslim world and, second, their thinking deviated so much from the viewpoint of the Shī'ites that it is difficult to count them among Muslims. What makes things easy is that the Khawārij ultimately became extinct and only one of their sects, called

Abāḍiyyah, has some followers today. The Abāḍiyyah were the most moderate of all the Khawārij, and that is the reason why they have survived.

The Bāṭinīs, too, have so liberally interfered in Islamic ideas on the basis of esotericism that it is possible to say that they have twisted Islam out of shape. For this reason the Muslim world is not prepared to consider them as one of the sects of Islam.

About thirty years ago when the Dār al-Taqrīb Bayna al-Madhāhib al-'Islāmiyyah was established in Cairo, the Imāmiyyah Shī'ā, the Zaydiyyah, the Ḥanafī, the Shāfi'ī, the Mālikī and the Ḥanbalī sects each had a representative. The Ismā'īlīs tried hard to send a representative of their own; but no such representative was accepted by other Muslims. Contrary to the Khawārij, who did not create a system of thought, the Bāṭinīs, despite their serious deviations, do have a significant school of *kalām* and philosophy. There have emerged among them important thinkers who have left behind a considerable number of works. Lately, Orientalists have been showering great attention on Bāṭinī thought and works.

One of the prominent Ismā'īlī figures is Nāṣir Khusraw al-'Alawī (d.841/1437–38), the well-known Persian poet and author of such famous works as *Jāmi' al-Ḥikmatayn*, *Kitāb wajh al-Dīn* and *Khuwān al-'Ikwān.* Another is Abū Ḥātam al-Rāzī (d. 332/943–44), the author of *A'lām al-Nubuwwah.* Others are Abū Ya'qūb al-Sijistānī, the author of *Kashf al-Maḥjūb* (its Persian translation has been recently published), who died during the second half of the 4th/10th century; Ḥamīd al-Dīn al-Kirmānī, a pupil of Abū Ya'qūb al-Sijistānī, who has written a large number of books about the Ismā'īlī faith; Abū Ḥanīfah Nu'mān ibn Thābit, well known as Qāḍī Nu'mān or 'the *Shī'ī* Abū Ḥanīfah' (i.e. Ismā'īlī); his knowledge of *fiqh* and *ḥadīth* is good, and his well-known book *Da'ā'im al-Islam* was printed by lithotype several years ago.

## Mu'tazilites

We shall begin our discussion – and we shall explain later why – with the Mu'tazilites. The emergence of this sect took place during the latter part of the first century or at the beginning of the second. Obviously *'ilm al-kalām*, like any other field of study, developed gradually and attained maturity slowly.

First we shall enumerate the principal Mu'tazilite beliefs, or rather, the basic and salient points of their school of thought. Second, we shall mention well-known Mu'tazilite figures and their role in history. Then we shall outline the transitions and changes in their thought and beliefs.

The Mu'tazilites hold many, not all confined to religious matters or to matters that they believe form an essential part of faith. They cover a number of physical, social, anthropological and philosophical issues, which are not directly related to the faith. However, there is a certain relevance of these problems to religion, and Mu'tazilites believe that any inquiry about the matters of religion is not possible without studying them.

There are five principal doctrines that, according to the Mu'tazilites themselves, constitute their basic tenets:

1. *Tawḥīd*, i.e. absence of plurality and attributes.

2. Justice (*'adl*), i.e. God is just and that He does not oppress His creatures.

3. Divine retribution (*al-wa'd wa al-wa'īd*), i.e. God has determined a reward for the obedient and a punishment for the disobedient, and there can be no uncertainty about it. Therefore, Divine pardon is possible only if the sinner repents, for forgiveness without repentance (*tawbah*) is not possible.

4. *Manzilah bayna al-manzilatayn* (a position between the two positions).

This means that a *fāsiq* (i.e. one who commits one of the 'greater sins', such as a wine drinker, adulterer or liar) is neither a believer (*mu'min*) nor an infidel (*kāfir*); *fisq* is an intermediary state between belief and infidelity.

*Al-amr bil ma'rūf wa al-nahy 'an al-munkar* (bidding to do what is right and lawful, and forbidding what is wrong and unlawful). The opinion of the Mu'tazilites about this Islamic duty is, first, that the *sharī'ah* is not the exclusive means of identifying the *ma'rūf* and the *munkar*; human reason can, at least partially, independently identify the various kinds of *ma'rūf* and *munkar*. Second, the implementation of this duty does not necessitate the presence of the Imām, and is a universal obligation of all Muslims, whether the Imām or leader is present or not.

Only some categories of it are the obligation of the Imām or ruler of Muslims, such as implementation of the punishments (*ḥudūd*) prescribed by the *sharī'ah*, guarding of the frontiers of Islamic countries and other such matters relating to the Islamic government.

Occasionally, the Mu'tazilite *mutakallimīn* have devoted independent volumes to discussion of their five doctrines, such as the famous *al-Uṣūl al-Khamsah* of al-Qāḍī 'Abd al-Jabbār al-Astarābādī (d. 415/ 1025), a Mu'tazilite contemporary of al-Sayyid al-Murtaḍā 'Alam al-Hudā and al-Ṣāḥib ibn 'Abbād (d. 100/995).

As can be seen, only the principles of *tawḥīd* and justice can be considered parts of the essential doctrine. The other three principles are significant only because they characterize the Mu'tazilites. Even Divine Justice - although the notion of it is definitely supported by the *Qur'an*, and belief in it is a necessary part of the Islamic faith and doctrine - has been made one of the five major doctrines because it characterizes the Mu'tazilites. Belief in Divine Knowledge and Power are as much an essential part of the Islamic faith and principal doctrine.

In the *shī'ī* faith also the principle of Divine Justice is considered one of the five essential doctrines. The question thus naturally arises: what is particular about Divine Justice that it should be counted among the essential doctrines, whereas justice is only one of the Divine Attributes? Is not God just in the same manner as He is the Omniscient, the Mighty, the Living, the Perceiver, the Hearer and the Seer? All those Divine

Attributes are essential to the faith. Then why is justice is given so much prominence among the Divine Attributes?

The answer is that justice has no advantage over other Attributes. The *shī'ī mutakallimīn* have specially mentioned justice among the principal *shī'ī* doctrines because the Ash'arites – who form the majority of the Ahl al-Sunnah – implicitly deny that it is an Attribute, whereas they do not reject the Attributes of knowledge, life, will, etc. Accordingly, justice is counted among the specific doctrines of the Shī'ites, as also of the Mu'tazilites. The above-mentioned five doctrines constitute the basic position of the Mu'tazilites from the viewpoint of *kalām*. But, as was said earlier, the Mu'tazilite beliefs are not confined to these five and cover a broad range from theology, physics and sociology to anthropology, in all of which they hold specific beliefs. Discussion of these lies outside the scope of this text.

## The Doctrine of *al-Tawḥīd*

*Tawḥīd* has various kinds and levels: *al-tawḥīd al-dhātī* (Unity of the Essence), *al-tawḥīd al-ṣifātī* (Unity of the Attributes, i.e. with the Essence), *al-tawḥīd al-af'ālī* (Unity of the Acts), *al-tawḥīd al-'ibādī* (monotheism in worship).

*Al-Tawḥīd al-dhātī* means that the Divine Essence is one and unique; it does not have a like or match. All other beings are God's creations and inferior to Him in station and in degree of perfection. In fact, they cannot be compared with Him. The idea of *al-tawḥīd al-dhātī* is made clear by the following two [Qur'anic] verses:

Nothing is like Him. (42:11)
He has no match [whatsoever]. (112:4)

*Al-tawḥīd al-ṣifātī* means that the Divine Attributes such as Knowledge, Power, Life, Will, Perception, Hearing, Vision, etc. are not realities separate from God's Essence. They are identical with the Essence, in the sense that the Divine Essence is such that the Attributes are true of It, or is such that It manifests these Attributes.

*Al-tawḥīd al-af'ālī* means that all beings, or rather all acts (even human acts) exist by the Will of God, and are in some way willed by His sacred Essence.

*Al-Tawḥīd al-'ibādī* means that no other being except God deserves worship and devotion. Worship of anything besides God is *shirk* (polytheism) and puts the worshipper outside the limits of Islamic *tawḥīd* or monotheism.

In a sense *al-tawḥīd al-'ibādī* (*tawḥīd* in worship) is different from other kinds of *tawḥīd*, because the first three relate to God and this kind relates to creatures. In other words, the Unity of Divine Essence, His Uniqueness and the identity of the Essence and Attributes, the unity of the origin of everything – all these are matters that relate to God. But *tawḥīd* in worship, i.e. the necessity of worshipping the One God, relates to the behaviour of creatures. In reality, of course, *tawḥīd* in worship is also related to God, because it means Uniqueness of God as the only deserving object of worship, and that He is in truth the One Deity Worthy of Worship. The statement '*lā ilāha illallāh*' encompasses all aspects of *tawḥīd*, although its first signification is monotheism in worship.

*Al-tawḥīd al-dhātī* and *al-tawḥīd al-'ibādī* are part of the basic doctrines of Islam. Any failure to adhere wholly to belief in these two principles would put one outside the pale of Islam. No Muslim has ever opposed these two basic beliefs.

Lately, the Wahhābīs, who are followers of Muḥammad ibn 'Abd al-Wahhāb, who in turn was a follower of Ibn Taymiyyah, a Ḥanbalī from Syria, have claimed that some common beliefs of the Muslims, such as a belief in intercession (*shafā'ah*), and some of their practices, such as invoking the assistance of the prophets (A.S.) and holy saints (R), are opposed to the doctrine of *al-tawḥīd al-'ibādī*. But these are not considered by other Muslims to conflict with. The point of difference between the Wahhabis and other Muslims is not whether anyone besides God – for instance the prophets or saints – is worthy of worship. There is no debate on this point. The debate is about whether the invoking of intercession and assistance can be considered a form of worship or not. Therefore, the difference is a secondary, not a primary one. Islamic scholars have rejected the viewpoint of the Wahhabis in elaborate, well-reasoned answers.

*Al-tawḥīd al-ṣifātī* (the Unity of Divine Essence and Attributes) is a point of debate between the Mu'tazilites and the Ash'arites. The latter deny it while the former affirm it. *al-tawḥīd al-af'ālī* is also another point of difference between them, only in this instance it is the Ash'arites who affirm it and the Mu'tazilites who deny it.

When the Mu'tazilites call themselves *ahl* al-*tawḥīd*,

and count it among their doctrines, they mean thereby *al-tawḥīd al-ṣifātī*, not *al-tawḥīd al-dhātī* nor *al-tawḥīd al-ʻibādī* (which are not disputed) nor *al-tawḥīd al-afʻālī*. This is because, first, they negate *al-tawḥīd al-afʻālī* and, second, they expound their own viewpoint about it under the doctrine of justice, their second article.

The Ashʻarites and the Muʻtazilites formed two radically opposed camps on the issues of *al-tawḥīd al-ṣifātī* and *al-tawḥīd al-afʻālī*. To repeat, the Muʻtazilites affirm *al-tawḥīd al-ṣifātī* and reject *al-tawḥīd al-afʻālī*, while the Ashʻarite position is the reverse. Both have advanced arguments in support of their positions. We shall discuss the *Shīʻī* position regarding these two aspects of *tawḥīd* in the relevant chapter.

## The Doctrine of Divine Justice

I have mentioned above the five fundamental Muʻtazilite principles and explained the first issue, i.e. their doctrine of *tawḥīd*. Here we shall take up their doctrine of Divine Justice.

Of course, it is evident that none of the Islamic sects denied justice as one of the Divine Attributes. No one has ever claimed that God is not just. The difference between the Muʻtazilites and their opponents is in the interpretation of justice. In the view of the Muʻtazilites, the interpretation of the Ashʻarites amounts to a denial of the Attribute of justice. The Ashʻarites themselves naturally have no desire to be considered the opponents of justice.

The Muʻtazilites believe that some acts are essentially 'just' and some intrinsically 'unjust.' For instance, rewarding the obedient and punishing the sinners is justice; and God is Just, i.e. He rewards the obedient and punishes the sinners, and it is impossible for Him to act otherwise. Rewarding the sinners and punishing the obedient is essentially and intrinsically unjust, and it is impossible for God to do such a thing. Similarly, compelling His creatures to commit a sin or creating them without any power of free will, then putting sinful acts into their hands and punishing them on account of those sins – this is injustice, an ugly thing for God to do; it is unjustifiable and unGodly. But the Ashʻarites believe that no act is intrinsically or essentially just or unjust. Justice is essentially whatever God does. If, supposedly, God were to punish the obedient and reward the sinners, it would be as just. Similarly, if God creates His creatures without any free will or freedom of action, then causes them to commit sins and punishes them – it is not essential injustice. If we suppose that God acts in this manner, it must be justice:

**Whatever Khusrow does is Sweet *(Shīrīn)*.**

For the same reason that the Muʻtazilites emphasize justice, they deny *al-tawḥīd al-afʻālī.* They say that *al-tawḥīd al-afʻālī* implies that God, not human beings, is the maker of human deeds. Since it is accepted that man attains reward and punishment in the hereafter, if God is the creator of human actions and yet punishes them for their evil deeds – which not they but God Himself has brought about – that would be injustice (*ẓulm*) and contrary to Divine Justice. Accordingly, the Muʻtazilites consider *al-tawḥīd al-af'ālī* to be contrary to the doctrine of justice.

Moreover, the Mu'tazilites are staunch believers in and defenders of human freedom and free will, unlike the Ash'arites who deny human freedom and free will.

Under the doctrine of justice – in the sense that some deeds are inherently just and some inherently unjust, and that human reason dictates that justice is good and must be practised, whereas injustice is evil and must be abstained from – they advance another general, more comprehensive doctrine, which is that 'beauty' (*ḥusn*) and 'ugliness' (*qubḥ*) or good and evil are inherent properties of acts. For instance, truthfulness, trustworthiness, chastity and fear of God are intrinsically good qualities, and falsehood, treachery, indecency and neglectfulness are intrinsically evil. Therefore, deeds in essence possess inherent goodness or evil, even before they come before the judgement of God.

This leads them to another doctrine about reason, namely, that human reason can independently judge (or perceive) the good or evil in things. The good or evil of some deeds can be judged by human reason independently of the commands of the *sharī'ah*. The Ash'arites oppose this view too.

The belief in the inherent good or evil of acts and the capacity of reason to judge them, upheld by the Mu'tazilites and rejected by the Ash'arites, brought many other problems in its wake, some of which were related to theology, some to human predicament; such as whether the Divine Acts or, rather, the creation of things has purpose or not. The Mu'tazilites claimed that absence of a purpose in the creation is *qabīḥ* (an ugly thing) and so rationally impossible. What about a duty that is beyond one's power to fulfil? Is it possible that God may burden someone with a duty that is beyond his capability? The Mu'tazilites considered this, too, to be *qabīḥ* and so impossible.

Is it within the power of a believer (*mu'min*) to turn apostate? Does the infidel (*kāfir*) have any power over his own infidelity (*kufr*)? The answer of the Mu'tazilites is in the affirmative; for if the believer and the infidel had no power over their belief and infidelity, it would be wrong (*qabīḥ*) to reward and punish them. The Ash'arites rejected Mu'tazilite doctrines entirely.

## Retribution *(al-Wa'd wa al-Wa'īd)*

*Wa'd* means the promise of reward and *wa'īd* means the threat of punishment. The Mu'tazilites believe that God does not break His own promises (all Muslims unanimously accept this) or renounce His threats, as the Qur'anic verse regarding Divine promise confirms:

> Indeed God does not break the promise. (13:31)

Accordingly (the Mu'tazilites say), all threats addressed to sinners and the wicked, such as the punishments declared for an oppressor, a liar or an imbiber of wine, will all be carried out without fail, except when the sinner repents before death. Therefore, pardon without repentance is not possible.

From the viewpoint of the Mu'tazilites, pardon without repentance implies failure to carry out the threats (*wa'īd*), and such an act, like the breaking of a promise (*khulf al-wa'd*), is *qabīḥ*, and thus impossible. Thus the Mu'tazilite beliefs regarding Divine retribution and Divine forgiveness are interrelated, and both arise from their belief in the inherent good and evil of deeds determinable by reason.

## *Manzilah Bayna al-Manzilatayn*

The Mu'tazilite belief in this matter emerged in the wake of two opposite beliefs in the Muslim world about the faith (*īmān*) or infidelity (*kufr*) of the *fāsiq*. For the first time the Khawārij maintained that committing any of the capital sins (*kabā'ir*) was contrary to faith (*īmān*) and equal to infidelity. Therefore, the perpetrator of a major sin is a *kāfir*.

As we know, the Khawārij emerged after the incident of arbitration (*taḥkīm*) during the Battle of Ṣiffīn about the year 37/657–58 under the caliphate of Amīr al-Mu'minīn 'Alī (A.S.). As the *Nahj al-Balāghah* tells us, Amīr al-Mu'minīn (A.S.) argued with them on this issue and refuted their viewpoint by numerous arguments. The Khawārij, even after 'Alī (A.S.), were against the caliphs of the period, and staunchly espoused the cause of *al-amr bi al-ma'rūf wa al-nahy 'an al-munkar*, denouncing others for their evil and calling them apostates and infidels. Since most of the caliphs indulged in the capital sins, they were naturally regarded as infidels by the Khawārij. Accordingly, they were adversaries of the current politics.

Another group that emerged (or was produced by the hands of vested political interests) was that of the Murji'ah, whose position with regard to the effect of capital sins was precisely opposite to that of the Khawārij. They held that faith and belief are a matter of the heart. One would remain a Muslim if one's faith – which is an inner affair of the heart – were intact; evil deeds cannot do any harm. Faith compensates for all wickedness.

The opinions of the Murji'ah were to the benefit of the rulers, and tended to make the people regard their wickedness and indecencies as unimportant, and even to consider them, despite their destructive character, as men worthy of paradise. The Murji'ah stated in unequivocal terms, 'The respectability of the station of the ruler is secure, no matter how much he may sin. Obedience to him is obligatory and prayers performed in his leadership are correct.' The tyrannical caliphs therefore backed them. For the Murji'ah, sin and wickedness, no matter how serious, are no detriment to one's faith; the perpetrator of the major sins is a *mu'min*, not a *kāfir*.

The Mu'tazilites took a middle path in this matter. They maintained that the perpetrator of a major sin is neither a *mu'min* nor a *kāfir*, but occupies a position in between, which they termed *manzilah bayna al-manzilatayn*.

It is said that the first to express this belief was Wāṣil ibn 'Aṭā', a pupil of al-Ḥasan al-Baṣrī. One day Wāṣil was sitting with his teacher, who was asked his opinion about the difference between the Khawārij and the Murji'ah on this issue. Before al-Ḥasan could say anything, Wāṣil declared, 'In my opinion a perpetrator of the major sins is a *fāsiq*, not a *kāfir*.' After this, he left the company or perhaps was expelled by al-Ḥasan al-Baṣrī – and as he went his own way he started propagating his own views. His pupil and brother-in-law 'Amr ibn 'Ubayd joined him. At this point Ḥasan declared, '*i'tazala 'annā*' ('He [Wāṣil] has departed from us'). According to another version, people said of Wāṣil and 'Amr, '*i'tazalā qawl al-ummah*' ('They have departed from the doctrines held by the *ummah*'), and that they had invented a third path.

## *Al-Amr bi al-Ma'rūf wa al-Nahy 'an al-Munkar*

*Al-amr bi al-ma'rūf wa al-nahy 'an al-munkar* is an essential Islamic duty, unanimously accepted by all Muslims. Differences occur only in the limits and conditions related to it.

For instance, the Khawārij believed in it without any limits and conditions whatsoever. They believed that this twofold duty must be performed in all circumstances. Others believed that the conditions of probability of effectiveness (*al-ma'rūf*) and absence of any dangerous consequences were necessary for this obligation to be applicable, whereas the Khawārij did not believe in any such restrictions. Some believed that it is sufficient to fulfil the duty of *al-amr wa al-nahy* with the heart and the tongue, i.e. one should support *al-ma'rūf* and oppose *al-*

*munkar* in one's heart and use one's tongue to speak up for *al-ma'rūf* and against *al-munkar*. But the Khawārij considered that the only right way to fulfil this duty was to take up arms and to unsheathe one's sword.

Opposed to them was a group who considered *al-amr wa al-nahy* to be subject to the above conditions and, moreover, that there was no need to go beyond the confines of the heart and the tongue to satisfy them. Aḥmad ibn Ḥanbal is counted among them. According to this group, a bloody uprising is not justified or permitted as a means of struggling against unlawful activities.

The Mu'tazilites accepted the conditions for *al-amr wa al-nahy*, but, not limiting it to the heart and the tongue, maintained that, if unlawful practices become common or if the state is oppressive and unjust, it is obligatory for Muslims to rise in armed revolt.

Thus the belief special to the Mu'tazilites in regard to *al-amr bi al-ma'rūf wa al-nahy 'an al-munkar* – which contrasts with the position of the Ahl al-Ḥadīth and the Ahl al-Sunnah – is the belief in the necessity to rise up in arms to confront corruption. The Khawārij too shared this view, with the difference pointed out above.

## Other Mu'tazilite Notions and Beliefs

Hitherto we have looked at the basic doctrines of the Mu'tazilites. But as we mentioned before, the Mu'tazilites raised many an issue and defended their opinions about them. Some of them related to theology, some to physics, some to sociology and some to the human situation. Of the theological issues, some related to general metaphysics (*umūr ʿāmmah*) and some to theology proper (*ilāhiyyāt bi al-maʿnā al-akhaṣṣ*).[8] Like all other *mutakallimīn*, the Muʿtazilites raised metaphysical questions so as to use them to prepare the ground for the discussion of theological issues, which are their ultimate objectives. Similarly discussions in the natural sciences were intended to serve an introductory purpose, that is, to prove some religious doctrines or to find answers to objections. Here we shall enumerate some of these beliefs, beginning with theology.

## Theology

(i) *Al-tawḥīd al-ṣifātī* (i.e. unity of the Divine Attributes)

(ii) *ʿAdl* (Divine Justice).

(iii) *The Holy Qur'an* (*kalām Allah*) is created (*kalām*, or speech, is an attribute of Act, not of the Essence).

(iv) The Divine Acts are caused and controlled by purposes (i.e. every Divine Act is for the sake of some beneficial outcome).

(v) Forgiveness without repentance is not possible (the doctrine of retribution, or *waʿd wa waʿīd*).

(vi) Pre-eternity (*qidam*) is limited to God (in this belief, they are challenged only by the philosophers).

(vii) Delegation of a duty beyond the powers of the *mukallaf* (*al-taklīf bimā lā yuṭāq*) is impossible.

(viii) The acts of creatures are not created by God for five reasons; the exercise of Divine Will does not apply to the acts of men.[9]

(ix) The world is created and is not pre-eternal (only philosophers are opposed to this view).

(x) God cannot be seen with the eyes, either in this world or in the Hereafter.

## Physics

(i) Physical bodies are made up of indivisible particles.

(ii) Smell relates to particles scattered in air.

(iii) Taste is nothing but the effect of particles.

(iv) Light is made up of particles scattered in space.

(v) Interpenetration of bodies is not impossible (this belief is attributed to some Mu'tazilites).

The leaping of particles (*ṭafrah*)[10] is not impossible (this belief, too, is attributed to some Mu'tazilites).

## Human Problems

(i) Man is free, endowed with free will; not predetermined (this question, the problem of the nature of human acts [whether created by God or man] and the problem of Divine Justice are all interrelated).

(ii) Ability (*istiṭā'ah*); that is, man has power over his own acts, before he performs them or desists from them.

(iii) The believer (*mu'min*) has the power to become an infidel and the infidel (*kāfir*) is able to become a believer.

(iv) A *fāsiq* is neither a *mu'min* nor a *kāfir*.

(v) Human reason can understand and judge some matters independently (without the prior need of guidance from the *sharī'ah*).

(vi) In the case of conflict between reason and ḥadīth, reason is to be preferred.

(vii) It is possible to interpret the *Qur'an* with the help of reason.

## Political and Social Problems

(i) *Al-amr bi al-ma'rūf wa al-nahy 'an al-munkar* is obligatory even if it necessitates the taking up of arms.

The leadership (*imāmah*) of the Rāshidūn Caliphs was correct in the order it occurred.

'Alī (A.S.) was superior to the Caliphs who preceded him (this is the view of some of the Mu'tazilites, not of all. The earlier Mu'tazilites – with the exception of Wāṣil ibn 'Aṭā' – considered Abū Bakr as the best, but the majority of the latter Mu'tazilites considered 'Alī (A.S.) to be superior).

(ii) Evaluation and criticism of the companions of the Prophet (S) and their deeds are permissible.

A comparative study and analysis of the state policies of 'Umar and 'Alī (A.S.).

These represent a sample of the issues touched on by the Mu'tazilites, which are far more numerous than those to which we have referred. In some of these problems, they were contradicted by the Ash'arites, in some by the philosophers, in some by the Khawārij and in some by the Murji'ah. The Mu'tazilites never submitted to Greek thought and did not accept Greek philosophy indiscriminately, which entered the Islamic world at the same time as the emergence and rise of the Mu'tazilites.

On the other hand, with great courage, they wrote books against philosophy and philosophers, boldly expressing their own opinions. The controversy between *mutakallimīn* and philosophers benefited both *kalām* and philosophy. Both of them made progress, and in the course of time came so close to each other that there remained no disagreement except on a few issues.

## Transitions in the History of the Mu'tazilites

Obviously, all the above-mentioned problems were not posed at one time or by any single individual. Rather, they were raised gradually by several individuals, expanding the scope of *'ilm al-kalām.*

Among these mentioned, apparently the oldest problem was that of free will and determinism, in which the Mu'tazilites, of course, adhered to the notion of free will. This is a problem that is posed in the *Qur'an.* That is, the *Qur'an* refers to this issue in such a way as to stimulate thought on the subject. Some verses clearly indicate that man is free, not coerced in any of his acts. On the other hand, there are verses that, with equal clarity, indicate that all things depend on the Divine Will.

Here it may be thought that these two types of verses contradict each other. Accordingly, some explained away the verses upholding free will and supported determinism and predestination, while others explained away the verses that refer to the role of Divine Will and Intention and came down on the side of human freedom and free will. There is in fact a third group who see no contradiction between those two sets of verses.[11]

Moreover, the controversy between freedom and fate is frequently taken up in the utterances of 'Alī (A.S.). Therefore, it is almost contemporaneous with Islam itself. However, the division of Muslims into two opposite camps, one siding with free will and the other with fate, took place in the second half of the first/seventh century.

It is said that the idea of free will was first put into circulation by Ghaylān al-Dimashqī and Ma'bad al-Juhanī. The Banū Umayyah were inclined to propagate the belief in fate and predestination among the people, because it served their political interests. Under the cover of this belief that 'everything is by the Will of God' (*āmannā bi al-qadar khayrihī wa sharrihī* – 'We believe in fate, whether it bring good or evil'), they justified their oppressive and illegitimate rule. As a result, they repressed any notions of free will or human freedom, and Ghaylān al-Dimashqī and Ma'bad al-Juhanī were both killed. During that period the supporters of the belief in free will were called '*qadariyyah*'.

However, the problem of the infidelity or otherwise of the evildoer (*kufr al-fāsiq*) had become a subject of controversy even before the issue of freedom and fate, because it was raised by the Khawārij during the first half of the first century about the time of the caliphate of 'Alī (A.S.). But the Khawārij did not defend this view in the fashion of the *mutakallimīn*. Only when the problem was raised among the Mu'tazilites, with the emergence of their doctrine of *manzilah bayn al-manzilatayn*, did it take on the colour of a problem of *kalām*.

The problem of fate and freedom (*jabr wa ikhtiyār*) automatically brought in its wake such other problems as these: the problem of Divine Justice; the rational and essential goodness or badness (*ḥusn wa qubḥ dhātī wa 'aqlī*) of things and acts; dependence of Divine Acts on purposes; the impossibility of burdening a person with a duty exceeding his capacities; and the like.

During the first half of the second/eighth century one Jahm ibn Ṣafwān (d. 128/745) voiced certain beliefs regarding the Divine Attributes. The writers of intellectual and religious history of Islam (*milal wa niḥal*), claim that the problem of *al-tawḥīd al-ṣifātī* (that the Divine Attributes are not separate from the Divine Essence – which the Mu'tazilites call their 'doctrine of *tawḥīd*') and the problem of *nafy al-tashbīh*, also called *aṣl al-tanzīh*, (which means that nothing can be likened to God) was expressed for the first time by Jahm ibn Ṣafwān, whose followers came to be called the 'Jahmiyyah'. The Mu'tazilites followed the Jahmiyyah in their doctrines of *tawḥīd* and *tanzīh*, in the same way as they followed the qadariyyah on the issue of free will. Jahm ibn Ṣafwān himself was a Jabrite (i.e. a supporter of fate or predestination). The Mu'tazilites rejected his view of fate but accepted his view of *tawḥīd*.

The foremost among the Mu'tazilites, who established Mu'tazilism (*al-i'tizāl*) as a school of thought was Wāṣil ibn 'Aṭā', who, as mentioned earlier, was a pupil of al-Ḥasan al-Baṣrī and who parted company with his teacher and established his own school. We mentioned above two different explanations of the source of the name Mu'tazilites. Another version is that the term '*mu'tazilite*' originally referred to a group of individuals who remained neutral during the events of the Battle of al-Jamal and the Battle of Ṣiffīn, such as Sa'd ibn Abī Waqqāṣ, Zayd ibn Thābit and 'Abdullāh ibn 'Umar.

Later, when the issue of the faith or infidelity of the *fāsiq* was raised by the Khawārij, Muslims divided into two camps. One group took the third path, dissociating itself from the rest and maintaining a position of indifference to their debates. They adopted a neutrality with regard to a theoretical problem just as did such people as Sa'd ibn Abī Waqqāṣ in the midst of the heated social political climate of their time. Consequently they were called '*Mu'tazilah* ', 'the indifferent', and the name became stuck permanently.

Wāṣil was born in the year 80/699 and died in 141/758–59. His views were limited to those on the negation of the Attributes (as distinct from the Essence of God), free will, *manzilah bayna al-manzilatayn*, *al-wa'd wa al-wa'īd* and opinions on some differences among the companions.

After Wāṣil came 'Amr ibn 'Ubayd, who extended and gave final shape to the views of Wāṣil. After him came 'Amr ibn Abī al-Hudhayl al-'Allāf and Ibrāhīm ibn Sayyār al-Naẓẓām. Abū al-Hudhayl and al- Naẓẓām are both considered eminent Mu'tazilites. *kalām* attained its philosophical tinge at their hands. Abū al-Hudhayl studied philosophical works and wrote books in refutation of them. Al-Naẓẓām presented certain views in the sphere of physics, and it was he who offered the view that bodies are constituted of atoms. Abū al-Hudhayl died, most probably, in the year 255/869, and al- Naẓẓām in 231/845–46. Al-Jāḥiẓ (159/775 to 254/868), the famous author of the *al-Bayān wa al-Tabyīn*, was another eminent Mu'tazilite of the third/ninth century.

During the rule of the Banū Umayyah, the Mu'tazilites did not have good relations with the ruling authorities. In the early days of the Banū al-'Abbās, they took on a neutral stand.[12] But under al-Ma'mūn, who was himself learned in literature, sciences and philosophy, they attracted the ruler's patronage. Al-Ma'mūn and after him al-Mu'taṣim and al-Wāthiq were staunch patrons of the Mu'tazilites and all three of these caliphs called themselves Mu'tazilites.

It was during this period that a heated controversy began that ultimately extended to all corners of the vast Islamic dominions of the period. The issue under debate was whether Speech is an attribute of the Divine Act or an attribute of the Essence. Whether it is created and temporal (*ḥadīth*) or uncreated and eternal (*qadīm*) like Divine Knowledge, Power and Life. The Mu'tazilites believed that the *Qur'an* is created (in time) and is therefore a creation of God (*makhlūq*) and so temporal. They also maintained that belief in the pre-eternity of the *Qur'an* amounted to infidelity (*kufr*).

Opponents of the Mu'tazilites, by contrast, believed in the pre-eternity and uncreatedness of the *Qur'an*. Al-

Ma'mūn (r. 198/813 to 218/833) sent out a circular saying that any believer in the pre-eternity of the *Qur'an* would be liable to punishment. Many persons were thrown into prison and subjected to torture.

Al-Mu'taṣim (r. 218/833 to 227/842) and al-Wāthiq (r. 227/842 to 232/847) also followed al-Ma'mūn's practice. One of those who went to prison during that time was Aḥmad ibn Ḥanbal. This policy remained in force until al-Mutawakkil assumed power (r. 232/847 to 247/861). Al-Mutawakkil was not inclined to favour the Mu'tazilites and most of the ordinary people were also opposed to them. As a result the Mu'tazilites and their admirers suffered a reverse and indeed persecutions and reprisals. In the purges that followed, much blood was shed and homes were ruined. The period is remembered by Muslims as *miḥnah* – times of adversity and trial.

The Mu'tazilites never recuperated after this and the field was left open forever for their opponents, the Ahl al-Sunnah and the Ahl al-Ḥadīth. Nevertheless, there appeared some prominent personalities even during the following periods of their decline, such as 'Abdulāh ibn Aḥmad Abū al-Qāsim al-Balkhī, well known as al-Ka'bī(d. 319/ 931); Abū 'Alī al-Jubba'ī (d. 303/915–16); Abū al-Hāshim al-Jubba'ī (d. 321/933) the son of Abū 'Alī al-Jubba'ī; Qāḍī 'Abd al-Jabbār (d. 415/1024); Abū al-Ḥasan al-Khaiyyāṭ; al-Ṣāḥib ibn 'Abbād, al-Zamakhsharī (d. 538/1144); and Abū Ja'far al-'Iskāfī.

## Ash'arites

As we have seen, the ideas and notions that led to the emergence of the Mu'tazilite school were born during the latter half of the first century of Hijrah. The Mu'tazilites characteristically used a kind of logical and rational method for understanding the basic doctrines of the Islamic faith. Obviously, the first condition for such an approach is belief in the freedom, independence and validity of reason. It is also true that people at large are not used to ratiocination and intellectual analysis and always tend to equate 'religiosity' with 'credulity' and intellectual submission to the apparent meanings of the Qur'anic verses and in particular of the *aḥādīth.* They tend to look on every attempt at independent and original interpretation as a kind of rebellion against religion, especially if the political climate supports this attitude, and more so if some religious scholars propagate such an outlook, particularly when they really believe in their literalist outlook and are inflexible and fanatical in practice. The attacks of the Akhbāris on the uṣūliyyūn and the *mujtahidūn*, and the attacks of some *fuqahā'* and *muḥaddithūn* against philosophers in the Islamic world had their roots in such thinking.[13]

The Mu'tazilites had a deep-rooted interest in understanding Islam and its propagation and defence against atheists, Jews, Christians, Magians, Sabaeans, Manichaeans and others. They even trained missionaries and dispatched them to various regions. Nevertheless, their existence was threatened by the literalists, who called themselves 'Ahl al-Ḥadīth' or 'Ahl al-Sunnah'. They were ultimately stabbed in the back and weakened and gradually became extinct.

Despite it all, until about the beginning of the fourth/tenth century, there existed no rival school of *kalām* that could challenge the Mu'tazilites. All opposition was based on the claim that the views of the Mu'tazilites were contrary to the externals of the *ḥadīth* and the Sunnah. The leaders of the Ahl al-Ḥadīth, such as Mālik ibn Anas and Aḥmad ibn Ḥanbal, basically considered any debate, inquiry or argument about matters of faith to be unlawful (*ḥarām*). Not only did the Ahl al-Sunnah lack any system of *kalām* challenging the Mu'tazilites, but they were also opposed to *kalām* itself.

About the late third/ninth century and the early fourth/tenth, a new phenomenon came into being, thanks to the appearance of a distinguished thinker who had received instruction in Mu'tazilite teachings under Qāḍī 'Abd al-Jabbār and had mastered them. He rejected Mu'tazilite tenets and inclined towards the doctrines of the Ahl al-Sunnah. Being a man of some genius and equipped with the tools used by the Mu'tazilites, he established all the doctrines of the Ahl al-Sunnah on a rational basis and gave them the form of a relatively closely-knit intellectual system. That distinguished person was Abū al-Ḥasan al-Ash'arī (d. circa 330/941–42). Al-Ash'arī – unlike his predecessors among Ahl al-Ḥadīth, such as Aḥmad ibn Ḥanbal – considered debate and argument and use of the tools of logic in the matter of the doctrines of the faith as permissible, citing evidence from the *Qur'an* and the Sunnah to support his claim. He wrote a treatise entitled '*Risālah fī Istiḥsān al-Khawḍ fī 'Ilm al-Kalām* ' ('A Treatise on the Appropriateness of Inquiry into *'Ilm al-Kalām*').[14]

It was at this point that the Ahl al-Ḥadīth split into two groups: the Ash'arites or followers of Abū al-Ḥasan al-Ash'arī, who considered *kalām* permissible; and the Ḥanbalīs or followers of Aḥmad ibn Ḥanbal, who considered it unlawful. As already mentioned, Ibn Taymiyyah, a Ḥanbalī, wrote a book on the unlawfulness of logic and *kalām*.[15] There was another reason why people began to detest the Mu'tazilites. It was the period of calamity, or *miḥnah*, and the Mu'tazilites, under the patronage of the caliph al-Ma'mūn, wanted to coerce the people into accepting their belief in the createdness of the *Qur'an*. Their attempt at regimentation brought bloodshed, imprisonment, torture and exile, which shook Muslim society. The people held the Mu'tazilites responsible for that havoc and accordingly regarded them with much disfavour.

These two causes contributed to the public welcome given to the emergence of the school of Ash'arism. After Abū al-Ḥasan al-Ash'arī, other distinguished personalities appeared in this school and strengthened its foundations. Among them were: Qāḍī Abū Bakr al-Bāqillānī (a contemporary of al-Shaykh al-Mufīd), who died in the year 403/1012–13; Abū Isḥāq al-Isfarā'yinī (who is considered to belong to the generation after al-Bāqillānī and al-Sayyid al-Murtaḍā ʻAlam al-Hudā); Imām al-Ḥaramayn al-Juwaynī, the teacher of al-Ghazālī; Imām Muḥammad al-Ghazālī, the author of *Iḥyā' ʻUlūm al-Dīn* himself (d. 505/1111–12); and Imām Fakhr al-Dīn al-Rāzī.

Of course, the Ashʻarite school underwent gradual changes and, particularly in the hands of al-Ghazālī, *kalām* somewhat lost its characteristic colour and took on the hue of *ʻirfān* (Sufism). Imām al-Rāzī brought it close to philosophy. After Khwājah Nāṣir al-Dīn al-Ṭūsī wrote his book *Tajrīd al-Iʻtizāl* more than ninety per cent of *kalām* took on a philosophical tone. After the publication of the *Tajrīd*, all *mutakallimīn* – including the Muʻtazilites and the Ashʻarites – followed the same path that had been trodden by that great philosopher and *shīʻī mutakallīm*.

For instance, the later works of *kalām* such as *al-Mawāqif wa* al-*Maqāṣid* and the commentaries written upon them were all in the same mould as the Tajrīd. In fact, it may be said that, the more time has elapsed since Abū al-Ḥasan al-Ashʻarī, the more the leading Ashʻarites have moved away from him, bringing his doctrines closer to the views of the Muʻtazilites or of the philosophers.

The following are the main doctrines of al-Ashʻarī, which are aimed at defending the basic principles of the Ahl al-Sunnah or attempting a rational justification of their beliefs.

(i) The Divine Attributes, contrary to the belief of the Muʻtazilites and the philosophers, are not identical with the Divine Essence.

(ii) The Divine Will is all-embracing. Divine Providence and predestination encompass all events (this belief, too, is contrary to the view held by the Mu'tazilites, though in agreement with those of the philosophers).

All evil, like good, is from God (of course, this view is a logical corollary, in al-Ash'arī's view of the above belief).

(iii) Man is not free in his acts, which are created by God (this belief, too, in al-Ash'arī's view, necessarily follows from the doctrine of the all-embracing nature of the Divine Will).

(iv) Acts are not intrinsically good or evil, i.e. *ḥusn* or *qubḥ* of deeds is not intrinsic, but determined by the *Sharī'ah.* The same is true of justice. What is 'just' is determined by the *sharī'ah,* not by reason (contrary to the belief of the Mu'tazilites).

(v) Grace (*luṭf*) and selection of the best for creation (*al-aṣlaḥ*) are not incumbent upon God (contrary to the belief of the Mu'tazilites).

Man's power over his actions does not precede them (there is no *istiṭā'ah qabl al-fi'l*), but is commensurate and concurrent with the acts themselves (contrary to the belief of the Muslim philosophers and the Mu'tazilites).

Absolute deanthropomorphism *(tanzīh muṭlaq*), in other words, absolute absence of similarity between God and others does not hold (contrary to the Mu'tazilite view).

(vi) Doctrine of acquisition. Man does not 'create' his own acts; rather he 'acquires' or 'earns' them (this is in justification of the Ahl al-Sunnah's belief in the creation of human acts by God).

Possibility of the beatific vision. God shall be visible to human eyes on the Day of the Resurrection (contrary to the view of the Mu'tazilites and the philosophers).

(vii) The *fāsiq* is a believer, or *mu'min* (contrary to the view of the Khawārij, who consider him *kāfir*, and contrary to the Mu'tazilite doctrine of *manzilah bayna al-manzilatayn*).

There is nothing wrong in God's pardoning someone without repentance. Similarly, nothing is wrong in God's subjecting a believer to chastisement (contrary to the Mu'tazilite position).

Intercession (*shafā'ah*) is justifiable (contrary to the Mu'tazilite position).

(viii) To tell a lie or break a promise is not possible for God.

(iv) The world is created in time (*ḥddīth*) (contrary to the view of the philosophers).

The *Qur'an* is pre-eternal (*qadīm*); however, this is true of *al-kalām al-nafsī* (meaning of the *Qur'an*), not *al-kalām al-lafẓī* – the spoken word (this is in justification of the Ahl al-Sunnah's belief in the pre-eternity of the *Qur'an*).

(x) The Divine Acts do not follow any purpose or aim (contrary to the view of the philosophers and the Mu'tazilites) It is possible that God may burden a person with a duty beyond his power (contrary to the belief of the philosophers and the Mu'tazilites).

Abū al-Ḥasan al-Ash'arī was a prolific writer and reportedly compiled more than two hundred books. As many as a hundred are mentioned in biographies, although most of those works have apparently perished. The most famous of his works is *Maqālāt al-Islāmiyyīn*, which has been published. It is a very disorderly and confused work. Another one printed is *al-Luma'*, and other of his works may perhaps also have appeared in print.

Abū al-Ḥasan al-Ash'arī is one of those individuals whose ideas, regrettably, exercised a great influence on the Islamic world. Nevertheless, later, his works were subjected to severe criticism by philosophers and the Mu'tazilites. Ibn Sīnā, in *al-Shifā*, has refuted many of his ideas without mentioning his name. Even some of his followers, such as Qāḍī Abū Bakr al-Bāqillānī and Imām al-Ḥaramayn al-Juwaynī, revised and modified his views about predestination and the createdness of (human) acts.

Imām Muḥammad al-Ghazālī, although an Ash'arite who to a great extent established and strengthened the Ash'arite doctrines, put them on a different foundation. Thanks to al-Ghazālī, *kalām* was brought closer to *'irfān* and Sufism. Mawlānā Muḥammad al-Rūmī, the author of the Mathnawī, is, in his own way, an Ash'arite; but his deep *ṣūfī* inclinations give a different colour to all the issues of *kalām*. Imām Fakhr al-Dīn al-Rāzī, who was familiar with philosophic thought, transformed al-Ash'arī's *kalām*, further strengthening it.

The triumph of the Ash'arite school cost the Muslim world dearly. Its triumph was the victory of the forces of stagnation over freedom of thought. Despite the fact that the battle between Ash'arism and Mu'tazilism is related to the *Sunnī* world, even the *shīʿī* world could not remain unaffected by some of the stultifying effects of Ashʿarism. This triumph has particular historical and social reasons behind it, and certain political events effectively contributed to it.

- As mentioned earlier, during the third/ninth century, the caliph al-Ma'mūn, himself an intellectual and a man of learning, rose to the support of the Muʿtazilites. After him al-Muʿtaṣim and al-Wāthiq also followed him until al-Mutawakkil assumed the caliphate. Al-Mutawakkil played a basic role in the victory of the Ahl al-Sunnah's doctrines, which acquired dialectic foundations after one hundred years at the hands of al-Ashʿarī. Had al-Mutawakkil's way of thinking been similar to that of his predecessors, Muʿtazilism would assuredly have had a different fate.

The rise of the Seljūq Turks to power in Iran was another effective factor in the triumph and propagation of the Ashʿarite ideas. The Seljūqs did not believe in the freedom of thought. They were the antithesis of the Buyids, some of whom were men of scholarship and literary merit. Shīʿism and Muʿtazilism flourished in the Buyid court. Ibn al-ʿAmīd and al-Ṣāḥib ibn ʿAbbād, the two learned ministers of the Buyids, were both anti-Ashʿarites.

It is not the intention here to support Muʿtazilite doctrines, and later we shall expose the feebleness of many of their beliefs. However, what deserves appreciation in the Muʿtazilites is their rational approach

– something that died out with them. As we know, a religion as rich and resourceful as Islam needs a *kalām* that has an unshakeable faith in the freedom of reason.

## The Shī'ite *Kalām*

Now we turn our attention, if only briefly, to the Shī'ite *kalām*. *kalām*, in the sense of logical and rational argument about the principal doctrines of Islam, has a special and distinguished place in the *shī'ī* tradition. The *shī'ī kalām* emerges from the core of Shī'ite *ḥadīth* but is also mixed with *shī'ī* philosophy. We have seen how, in the early centuries, the Ahl al-Sunnah considered *kalām* to be inimical to the Sunnah and the *ḥadīth*. In fact, the opposite is true: the Shī'ite *kalām* is firmly rooted in the Sunnah and the *ḥadīth*. The reason is that the Shī'ite *ḥadīth*, unlike the *Sunnī* corpus on *ḥadīth*, consists of numerous traditions in which profound metaphysical or social problems have been dealt with logically and analysed rationally. In the *Sunnī* corpus such analytic treatment of these subjects is missing. For instance, wherever there is mention of such matters as Divine Providence and Preordination, the all-embracing Will of the Almighty, the Divine Names and Attributes, the soul, life after death, the final reckoning, the *ṣirāṭ*, the balance or such issues as *imāmah*, *khilāfah* and the like, argument and rational explanation are absent. But in the *shī'ī* corpus on *ḥadīth*, all such issues are dealt with in a rational and discursive manner. A comparison between the list of the chapters of the six *Ṣiḥāḥ* and that of al-

Kulaynī's *al-Kāfī* will make this quite clear.

Accordingly, *kalām*, in the sense of rational and analytical treatment of problems, is found in the *shī'ī ḥadīth*. This is the reason why the Shī'ites were not divided; whereas the *Sunnīs* were divided into the 'Ahl al-Ḥadīth' and the 'Ahl al-kalām'.

We stated above, on the basis of the *Sunnī* textual sources, that the first doctrinal issue to become a subject of controversy was the issue of the *kufr* of a *fāsiq*, brought up by the Khawārij during the first half of the first century. Then there emerged the problem of freedom and fate, which was raised and argued by two individuals named Ma'bad al-Juhanī and Ghaylān al-Dimashqī. The belief they professed in this matter was contrary to the one held and propagated by the Umayyad rulers. Then, during the first half of the second century, the notion of the unity of Divine Attributes and Essence was posed by Jahm ibn Ṣafwān. There followed Wāṣil ibn 'Aṭā' and 'Amr ibn 'Ubayd, the founders of the Mu'tazilite school, who adopted the belief in free will from Ma'bad and Ghaylān and the doctrine of the Unity of Divine Essence and Attributes from Jahm ibn Ṣafwān, and themselves invented the doctrine of *manzilah bayna al-manzilatayn* in the issue of the faith or infidelity of *fāsiq*. In so doing, they initiated debates in some other issues and thus were responsible for founding the first school in Islamic *kalām*.

This is how Orientalists and scholars of Islam in the West and the East explain and interpret the origins of rational speculation and debate in the Islamic world. This group, whether by accident or design, ignores the profound rational and demonstrative arguments advanced for the first time by Amīr al-Mu'minīn 'Alī (A.S.). The truth is that it was 'Alī (A.S.), in his sermons and discussions, who introduced the rational approach to Islamic teachings and initiated profound discussion on the subjects of Divine Essence and Attributes, temporality (*ḥudūth*) and pre-eternity (*qidam*), simplicity (*bisāṭah*) and compositeness (*tarkīb*), unity (*waḥdah*) and plurality (*kathrah*), etc. These are recorded in the *Nahj al-Balāghah* and other authentic texts of *shī'ī ḥadīth*. The discussions have a colour, flavour and spirit that are totally distinct from the approaches of the Mu'tazilites and the Ash'arites to the controversies of *kalām*, or even from that of the Shī'ites scholars, who were influenced by their contemporary *kalām*.

I have discussed this matter in *Sayrī dar Nahj al-Balāghah* ('A Journey through the *"Nahj al- Balāghah"*') and in the preface to Vol. V of *Uṣūl-e Falsafah wa Rawishe Ri'ālism*.

*Sunnī* historians confess that from the earliest days the Shī'ite thinking was philosophical in approach. The Shī'ite intellectual and theoretical approach is opposed not only to Ḥanbalī thinking – which fundamentally rejects the idea of using discursive reasoning in religious belief – and the Ash'arite approach – which denies the independence of reason and subordinates it to literalist appearance – but also to Mu'tazilite thinking with all its predilection for reason. Because, although Mu'tazilite thought is rational, it is dialectical or polemical (*jadalī*), not discursive or demonstrative (*burhānī*).

In our discussion of the basics of Islamic philosophy, where we looked at the difference between peripatetic (*ḥikmat al-mashshā'*) and illuminationist (*ḥikmat al-ishrāq*) philosophies, we also explained the difference between dialectical (Mu'tazilite and Ash'arite) *kalām* and mystical or intuitive approaches to philosophical issues.[16] The reason why most Islamic philosophers have been Shī'ites is that only the Shī'ites have preserved and kept Islamic philosophy alive, since they acquired this spirit from their Imāms (A.S.), particularly from the first Imām, Amīr al-Mu'minīn 'Alī (A.S.).

The *shī'ī* philosophers, without having to mould philosophy into *kalām* and without transforming rational philosophy into dialectical philosophization, consolidated the doctrinal basis of Islam under the inspiration of the Qur'anic Revelation and the guiding principles of their spiritual leaders. If we wish to enumerate the *Shī'ī mutakallimīn*, that is, those who have applied rational thought to the doctrines of the Faith, we shall have to include a group of *muḥaddithūn* as well as a group of *Shī'ī* philosophers among them. This is because, as was said earlier, both Shī'ite *ḥadīth* and Shī'ite philosophy have accomplished the function of *'ilm al-kalām* to a greater extent than *kalām* itself.

But if by *mutakallimīn* we mean only those who, under Mu'tazilite or Ash'arite influence, resorted to the tools of dialectical reasoning, we are forced to select only a particular group of them. However, there is no reason to concentrate our attention on this particular group only.

If we discount the utterances of the infallible Imāms (A.S.) about doctrines, delivered in the form of sermons, narratives or prayers, the first *shīʿī* writer to compile a book on doctrines of faith was ʿAlī ibn Ismāʿīl ibn Maytham al-Tammār. Maytham al-Tammār himself was an orator and expert debater, and was one of the closest companions of Amīr al-Mu'minīn ʿAlī (A.S.). ʿAlī ibn Ismāʿīl was his grandson. He was a contemporary of ʿAmr ibn ʿUbayd and Abū al-Hudhayl al-ʿAllāf, the famous figures of *kalām* during the first half of the second century, who were from the first generation of the founders of Muʿtazilite *kalām.*

Among the companions of al-Imām al-Ṣādiq (A.S.), there is a group of individuals, referred to as *mutakallīm* by the Imām (A.S.) himself, who included Hishām ibn al-Ḥakam, Hishām ibn Sālim, Ḥamrān ibn Aʿyan, Abū Jaʿfar al-Aḥwal (known as Mu'min al-Ṭāq), Qays ibn Māṣir and others.

(A) Al-Kāfī relates the story of a debate between this group and an opponent in the presence of al-Imām al-Ṣādiq (A.S.), which pleased him. This group lived during the first half of the second century, and was trained in the school of al-Imām al-Ṣādiq (A.S.). This shows that the Imāms of the Ahl al-Bayt (A.S.) not only themselves engaged in discussion and analysis of the problems of *kalām* but also trained some of their pupils for the express purpose of conducting such debates and arguments. Of these Hishām ibn al-Ḥakam distinguished himself only in *'ilm al-kalām*, not in *tafsīr*, *fiqh* or *ḥadīth*. Al-Imām al-Ṣādiq used to treat him with more respect than the others, even when he was a raw youth, and used to offer him a preferred seat, all because of his expertise in *kalām*.

By showing preference for Hishām the *mutakallīm* over other pupils who were experts in *ḥadīth* and *fiqh*, al-Imām al-Ṣādiq (A.S.), in fact, hoped to raise the status of *kalām* as against *ḥadīth* and *fiqh*. Obviously, this played a decisive role in the promotion of *'ilm al-kalām* and consequently gave *Shī'ī* thought a dialectical and philosophical character.

(B) Al-Imām al-Riḍā (A.S.) personally participated in debates in which al-Ma'mūn invited *mutakallimīn* of various schools to take part. The records of such meetings are preserved in the *Shī'ī* texts.

It is indeed amazing that Orientalists should be completely silent about all such events pertaining to the efforts of Amīr al-Mu'minīn 'Alī (A.S.) and ignore the role of the Infallible Imāms (A.S.) in the revival of rational inquiry in matters of religious doctrine.

(C) Faḍl ibn Shādhān al-Nīshābūrī, a companion of al-Imām al-Riḍā (A.S.), al-Imām al-Jawād (A.S.) and al-Imām al-Hādī (A.S.), whose tomb is in Nīshābūr, apart from being a *faqīh* and a *muḥaddith*, was also a *mutakallīm*. He is reported to have written a large number of books.

The Nawbakht family produced many illustrious personalities, most of whom were *mutakallimīn*. Faḍl ibn Abī Sahl ibn al-Nawbakht, a contemporary of Hārūn, was attached to the famous Bayt al-Ḥikmah library and well known as a translator from Persian into Arabic; Isḥāq ibn Abī Sahl ibn al-Nawbakht; his son, Ismā'īl ibn Isḥāq ibn Sahl ibn al-Nawbakht; another of his sons, 'Alī ibn Isḥāq; his grandson, Abū Sahl Ismā'īl ibn 'Alī ibn Isḥāq ibn Abī Sahl ibn al-Nawbakht (called '*shaykh al-mutakallimīn*' of the Shī'ites); Ḥasan ibn Mūsā al-Nawbakht, a nephew of Ismā'īl ibn 'Alī; and several others of this family were all *Shī'ī mutakallimīn.*

(D) Ibn Qibah al-Rāzī in the third/ninth century and Abū 'Alī ibn Miskawayh, the famous doctor of medicine and author of *Tahdhīb al-Akhlāq wa Taṭhīr al-A'rāq* , who lived during the early fifth/eleventh century, are also *shī'ī mutakallimīn.*

The *shī'ī mutakallimīn* were many in number. Khwājah Nāṣir al-Dīn al-Ṭūsī, the famous philosopher and mathematician and author of the *Tajrīd al-I'tiqād*, and al-'Allāmah al-Ḥillī, the well-known *faqīh* and commentator of the *Tajrīd al-I'tiqād* , were well-known *mutakallimīn* of the seventh/thirteenth century.

Khwājah Nāṣir al-Dīn al-Ṭūsī, himself a learned philosopher, created the most solid work of *kalām* in the *Tajrīd al-I'tiqād* , which has always attracted the attention of all *mutakallimīn*, whether *shī'ī* or *sunnī.* Al-Ṭūsī has, to a great extent, brought *kalām* out of the dialectical labyrinth and made it closer to discursive (rational) philosophy. In later times, *kalām* almost completely lost its dialectical form and thinkers abandoned dialectical philosophy in favour of discursive (rational) philosophy.

The Shī'ite philosophers after al-Ṭūsī brought the essential problems of *kalām* into philosophy and applied philosophical methods of inquiry to the study and analysis of these problems, with greater success than had been attained by the *mutakallimīn* who employed older methods. For example, Mullā Ṣadrā and Mullā Hādī Sabzawārī, though not usually counted among *mutakallimīn*, have been far more influential in Islamic thought than any of the true *mutakallimīn* themselves.

If we compare their approach to that of the basic Islamic texts, such as the *Qur'an*, the *Nahj al- Balāghah* and the prayers and traditions transmitted from the Ahl al-Bayt (A.S.), we find this approach and style of reasoning to be closer to that of the original teachers of the faith.

## The *Shī'ī* Standpoint

Here we shall briefly explain Shī'ite views on the issues current among Muslim *mutakallimīn*. Earlier, when we looked at the Mu'tazilite viewpoint, we noted that the Mu'tazilites considered their five doctrines,viz.*tawḥīd*, *'adl*, *al-wa'd wa al-wa'īd*, *manzilah bayna al-manzilatayn* and *al-'amr bi al-ma'rūf wa al-nahy 'an al-munkar*, to be fundamental to their school of thought. We said also that the reason for giving prominence to these doctrines above all other Mu'tazilite beliefs is that they characterize their school and distinguish it from the schools of their opponents. We should not construe from this that the five principles constitute the basic doctrines of the faith (*uṣūl al-Dīn*) of the Mu'tazilites and that all the remaining beliefs are regarded as subsidiary.

The Shī'ite scholars – not the Shī'ite Imāms (A.S.) – from the earliest days also introduced five doctrines, which they held to be characteristic of Shī'ism. They were: *tawḥīd*, *'adl*, *nubuwwah*, *imāmah* and *ma'ād* (Resurrection). It is generally said that these five are the basic tenets of the faith (*uṣūl al-Dīn*) and the rest have a subordinate significance, or are *furū' al-Dīn*. If by *uṣūl al-Dīn* we mean the doctrines in which it is essential to believe in order to be a Muslim, their number falls to two, namely, *tawḥīd* and *nubuwwah*. These are the only two beliefs contained in the Shahādatayn ( *ashhadu an lā ilāha illallāh wa ashhadu anna Muḥammadan rasūlullāh*). Moreover, the second testimony is related in particular to the prophethood of Muḥammad (S), not to prophethood in general, and the prophethood of other prophets is not covered by it. However, belief in the prophethood of all the other prophets (A.S.) is a part of the *uṣūl al-Dīn* and faith in it is compulsory for all believers.

If by *uṣūl al-Dīn* we mean the doctrines in which it is essential to have faith, as they form part of the totality of Islamic faith, then the number increases to include other matters such as belief in the existence of angels – which is explicitly stated in the *Qur'an*.[17] Furthermore, what is special about the Attribute of *'adl* (justice) that only this Divine Attribute should be included in the essential doctrine, to the exclusion of all other attributes, such as

Knowledge, Life, Power, Hearing or Vision? If belief in the Divine Attributes is necessary, it should be necessary to believe in all of them; if not, none of them ought to be made the basis of the faith.

Actually, the fivefold principles were selected in such a manner as, to determine certain tenets essential to the Islamic faith, on the one hand, and to specify the particular identity of the school, on the other. The doctrines of *tawḥīd*, *nubuwwah* and *ma'ād* are the three in which it is essential for every Muslim to believe. These three are, in other words, part of the objectives of Islam, the doctrine of *'adl* being the specific mark of the Shī'ite school.

The doctrine of *'adl*, although it is not part of the main objectives of the Islamic faith – in the sense that it does not differ from the other articles of faith pertaining to Knowledge, Life, Power, etc. – is one of those doctrines that represent the specific *shī'ī* outlook with regard to Islam.

The article on *imāmah*, from the Shī'ite viewpoint, covers both these aspects, i.e. it is a part of the essential doctrines and it also characterizes the Shī'ite school.

If faith in the existence of angels is also, on the authority of the *Qur'an*, essential and obligatory, then why was it not stated as a sixth article of the faith? The answer is that the above-mentioned articles are part of the objectives of Islam. That is, the Holy Prophet (S) called the people to believe in them. This means that the mission of the Prophet (S) prepared the ground for the establishment of these beliefs. But the belief in angels or in obligatory duties such as prayer and fasting is not a part of the objectives of the prophethood; it rather forms an essential accessory to it. In other words, such beliefs are essential accessories of faith in prophethood, but are not the objectives of prophethood.

The issue of *imāmah*, if viewed in socio-political terms or from the point of view of government and leadership, is similar to that of *'adl*, in that it is not an essential part of the faith. However, if viewed from a spiritual viewpoint – that is, recognizing that the Imām, to use the terminology of *ḥadīth*, is the *ḥujjah* (proof) of God and His *khalīfah* (vicegerent), who at all times serves as a spiritual link between every individual Muslim and the perfect human being – then it is to be considered as one of the articles of faith.

Now let us look separately at each of the particular doctrines of Shī'ite *kalām*, including the above-mentioned five doctrines.

### (i) *Tawḥīd*

*Tawḥīd* is one of the five doctrines of the Mu'tazilites, as also of the Ash'arites, with the difference that in the case of the Mu'tazilites it specifically means *al-tawḥīd al-ṣifātī*, which is denied by the Ash'arites. On the other hand, the specific sense of this term as affirmed by the Ash'arites is *al-tawḥīd al-af'ālī*, which is rejected by the Mu'tazilites.

As mentioned above, *al-tawḥīd al-dhātī* and *al-tawḥīd al-'ibādī*, since they are admitted by all, are outside the scope of our discussion. The concept of *tawḥīd* upheld by the Shī'ites, in addition to *al-tawḥīd al-dhātī* and *al-tawḥīd al-'ibādī*, also includes *al-tawḥīd al-ṣifātī* and *al-tawḥīd al-af'ālī.* That is, in the controversy regarding the Attributes, the Shī'ites are on the side of *al-tawḥīd al-ṣifātī*, and in the debate on human acts, they are on the side of *al-tawḥīd al-af'ālī.* Nevertheless, the *shī'ī* concept of *al-tawḥīd al-ṣifātī* is different from that of the Mu'tazilites. Also, their notion of *al-tawḥīd al-af'ālī* differs from that of the Ash'arites.

The Mu'tazilites concept of *al-tawḥīd al-ṣifātī* is synonymous with the idea of the absence of all Attributes from the Divine Essence or, to put it another way, with the concept that the Divine Essence is devoid of all qualities. But the *shī'ī* notion of *al-tawḥīd al-ṣifātī* means identity of the Attributes with the Divine Essence.[18] For further elaboration of this issue one must have recourse to works on Shī'ite *kalām* and philosophy.

The *Shī'ī* conception of *al-tawḥīd al-af'ālī* differs from the one held by the Ash'arites. The Ash'arite notion of *al-tawḥīd al-af'ālī* means that no creature is of any consequence in the scheme of things and everything is directly ordained by God. Accordingly, He is also the direct creator of the deeds of human beings and they are not creators of their own acts. Such a belief is similar to the idea of absolute predestination and has been refuted through many an argument. However, the notion of *al-tawḥīd al-af'ālī* upheld by the Shī'ites means that the system of causes and effects is real, and every effect, while being dependent on its proximate cause, is also dependent on God. These two modes of dependence do not operate in parallel but in series. For further clarification of this subject see my book *Insān wa sarnewisht* ('Man and Destiny').

### (ii) *'Adl*

The doctrine of *'adl* is common to both the Shī'ites and the Mu'tazilites. *'Adl* means that God bestows His mercy and blessings and so also His trials and chastisement according to the prior and intrinsic deservedness of beings, and that Divine mercy and trial, reward and punishment are determined in accordance with a particular order or law (which is also of Divine origin).

The Ash'arites deny this notion of *'adl* and such an order. In their view, belief in *'adl* in the sense of a just order necessitates God's subjection and subordination to something else and thus contradicts His Absolute Power. *'Adl* in itself implies several corollaries, to which we shall refer while explaining other doctrines.

### (iii) Free Will and Freedom

The *shī'ī* doctrine of free will is to some extent similar to that of the Mu'tazilites. But the two differ with regard to its meaning. Human freedom or free will for the Mu'tazilites is equivalent to Divine Resignation (*tafwīḍ*), i.e. leaving man to his own devices and suspending the Divine Will from any effective role. Of course, this is impossible, as has been shown.

Freedom and free will, in the understanding of the Shī'ites, mean that men are created as free beings. But they, like any other creature, are entirely dependent on the Divine Essence for their existence and all its multifarious modes, including the mode of action, all of which are derived from and dependent on God's merciful care, and they seek help from His Will.

Accordingly, free will and freedom in Shī'ism occupy an intermediate position between the Ash'arite (absolute) predestination (*jabr*) and the Mu'tazilite doctrine of freedom (*tafwīḍ*). This is the meaning of the famous dictum of the Infallible Imāms (A.S.), '*lā jabra wa lā tafwīḍ, Bal amrun bayna 'amrayn*' (Neither *jabr* nor *tafwīḍ*, but something intermediate between the two [extreme] alternatives).

The doctrine of free will is a corollary to the doctrine of Divine Justice.

### (iv) Inherent Morality or Immorality of Deeds (*Ḥusn wa Qubḥ Dhātī*)

The Mu'tazilites believe that all deeds are inherently and intrinsically either good or evil. For example, justice is intrinsically good and oppression is inherently evil. The wise man selects the good works and abstains from bad deeds. And since God the Almighty is Wise His Wisdom necessitates that He should do good and abstain from evil. Thus the inherent goodness or badness of acts, on the one hand, and the Wisdom of God, on the other, inevitably make some acts 'obligatory' for God and some 'undesirable'.

The Ash'arites are strongly opposed to this belief. They deny both the inherent goodness or badness of acts and the applicability of such judgements as 'obligatory' or 'undesirable' to God.

Some *shīʿī* thinkers, under the influence of the Muʿtazilite *kalām*, accepted the Muʿtazilite view in its above-mentioned form, but others, with greater insight, while accepting the doctrine of inherent morality or immorality of acts, rejected the view that the judgements of permissibility or undesirability are applicable to the Divine realm.[19]

### (v) Grace (*Luṭf*) and Choice of the Best *(Intikhāb al-Aṣlaḥ)*

There is a controversy between the Ashʿarites and the Muʿtazilites as to whether or not Grace or 'choice of the best' for the good of human beings is a principle that governs the universe. The Muʿtazilites considered Grace as a duty and obligation incumbent upon God. The Ashʿarites denied Grace and 'choice of the best.'

However, the principle of Grace is a corollary to the doctrine of justice and the doctrine of the innate goodness or badness of deeds. Some Shīʿite *mutakallimīn* have accepted the doctrine of Grace in its Muʿtazilite form, but others who consider it absolutely wrong to apply the notion of 'duty' and 'obligation' to God, advance another version of the doctrine of the 'choice of the best'. Space does not allow us to elaborate this here.

### (vi) Independence and Validity of Reason

Shīʿism affirms a greater independence, authority and validity for reason than the Muʿtazilites.

According to certain indisputable traditions of the

Ma'ṣūmūn (A.S.), reason is the internalized prophetic voice in the same way as a prophet is reason externalized. In the Shī'ite *fiqh*, reason (*'aql*) is considered one of the four valid primary sources of the Law.

## (vii) 'Aim' and 'Purpose' of Divine Acts

The Ash'arites reject the notion that the Divine Acts may be for one or several purposes or aims. They state that possession of a purpose or goal is solely applicable to man and other similar creatures. But God is above such matters, since having a purpose and aim implies subjection of a doer to that purpose or aim. God is free from and above every kind of limit, restriction and subordination, even though it be the limit imposed by a purpose.

The Shī'ites affirm the Mu'tazilite belief with regard to purposiveness of Divine Acts. They believe that there is a difference between the purpose of the act and the purpose of the doer. What is impossible is that God may seek to satisfy some purpose of His own through His Acts; however, a purpose or aim that is directed to the benefit of a creature is not at all incompatible with Divine perfection and the supremacy of His self-sufficing Essence.

The Possibility of *badā'* (Divine Abrogation of Predestiny) *badā'* is possible in Divine Acts, in the same way as it occurs in the abrogation of the Divinely decreed laws. An elaborate and satisfactory study of the issue of *badā'* may be found in such profound philosophical books as *al-Asfār*.

**(viii) Vision *(Ru'yah)* of God**

The Muʻtazilites vehemently deny the possibility of seeing God with the eyes. They believe that one may only have faith in the existence of God, a firm conviction in the depth of one's soul and mind, but that this is the highest faith that one may attain. The *Qur'an* lends credence to this belief:

> The sights do not perceive Him, and He perceives the sights, and He is All-subtle [incapable of being perceived] and All-knowing [i.e. He perceives the eyes and the rest of things]. (6:103)

The Ashʻarites, with equal vehemence, assert that God can be seen with the eyes, but only on the Day of Resurrection. They also cite as evidence certain Qur'anic verses and prophetic traditions, including the following:

> [Some] faces on that Day shall be bright, looking towards their Lord.(75:22–23)

The Shīʻites believe that God can never be seen with the eyes, neither in this life nor in the hereafter. Nevertheless, the highest kind of faith is not an intellectual one. Intellectual faith is *ʻilm al-yaqīn.* A higher level of faith is *ʻayn al-yaqīn* – certitude of the heart. *ʻAyn al-yaqīn* (literally 'certitude by sight') means witnessing God with the heart, not with the eyes. Thus, God is 'visible' to the heart. ʻAlī (A.S.) was once asked, 'Have you seen God?' He replied, 'I have not worshipped a god whom I have not seen. But He is visible to the hearts, not to the eyes.' The Imāms (A.S.) were asked whether the Prophet (S) saw God during his Ascension (*mi'rāj*). Their reply was, 'With the eyes? No. With the heart? Yes.' In this matter only the *ṣūfis* share a similar position to that of the Shī'ites.

### (ix) The Faith or Infidelity of the *Fāsiq*

On this issue, which has been referred to earlier, the *shī'ī* position coincides with that of the Ash'arites, but differs from that of the Khawārij (who believe that a *fāsiq* is *kāfir*) and the Mu'tazilites (who believe in *manzilah bayna al-manzilatayn*).

### (x) The Infallibility *('Iṣmah)* of the Prophets and the Imāms

This belief is characteristic of the Shī'ites, who hold that the prophets and the Imāms (A.S.) are infallible and do not commit any major or minor sin whatsoever.

### (xi) Forgiveness (*Maghfirah*) and Intercession (*Shafā'ah*)

On this issue also the Shī'ites differ from the cut-and-dried Mu'tazilite position that anybody who dies without repentance cannot possibly receive Divine forgiveness or (the Prophet's) intercession. Similarly, their position is also at variance with the indulgent and extravagant notion of *shafā'ah* held by the Ash'arites.[20]

## Notes

1. See, Murtaḍā Muṭahharī, *Sayrī dar Nahj al-Balāghah*, 69–76, where the author discusses the difference between the approach of the *Nahj al-Balāghah* to the problems of theology and metaphysics and the approach of Muslim *mutakallimīn* and philosophers to such problems.
2. *Zanādiqah* (sing. *zindīq*), a term applied heterogeneously and relatively, is used to describe any heretical group whose belief deviates radically from Islamic doctrines. The author probably uses the term to refer to one or more of such sects as the *Mu'aṭṭilah*, who denied the Creation and the Creator, reducing the world to an unstable mixture of the four elements, the Mānawiyyah (Manichaeans); and Mazdakiyyah, who were dualists, etc.
3. See, Murtaḍā Muṭahharī, *Insān wa sarnewisht* ('Man and Destiny').
4. See, Murtaḍā Muṭahharī, *'Adl-e Ilāhī* ('Divine Justice'), Introduction, 7–43.
5. Translator's note: There are at least seventy-five places where the various derivatives of the root *kalimah* occur in the *Qur'an*. In three places the phrase *Kalām Allah* is used in reference to the *Qur'an* (2:75, 9:6 &

48:15). The word *kalimah* ('word', 'statement') or the plural *kalimah* with reference to God occurs at least thirty times in the *Qur'an*, twice with reference to Jesus (A.S.) who is called a '*kalimah*' of God. The Gospel of John designates Jesus Christ (A.S.) as the 'Eternal Word of God'. The *Qur'an* also speaks of Jesus as a Word of God, while according to John's Gospel he is the Word, eternal and uncreated: 'Before the world was created, the Word already existed; he was with God, and he was the same as God.' We are further told: 'Through him God made all things, not one thing in all creation was made without him. The Word was the source of life . . . the Word became a human being and, full of grace and truth, lived among us. We saw his glory, the glory that he received as the Father's only Son.'

Probably the Christian belief in Jesus as the uncreated *kalimah* Allah (Word of God), some kind of a demiurge – a belief that probably emerged as a result of Manichaean influence on early Christianity – had prompted the early Muslims, engaged in polemics with Christians on the nature of Jesus Christ, to consider, in their turn, the *Qur'an*, the *Kalām* Allah, as uncreated and eternal.

6. 'Allāmah Sayyid Muḥammad Ḥusayn Ṭabāṭabā'ī, *Uṣūl-e Falsafah wa Rawishe Ri'ālism* ('The Principles and Method of Realism'), vol. V, chapter XIV, Introduction by Murtaḍā Muṭahharī, who has written very elaborate footnotes to the text of 'Allāmah Ṭabāṭabā'ī's book.
7. 'Abdurraḥmān al-Badawī, *Al-Madhāhib al-'Islāmiyyīn*, vol. I, p. 34. Apparently, the author does not number the *Ṭaḥāwiyyah*, the Māturīdiyyah and the Ẓāhiriyyah among the major schools of *kalām* or important enough to be included in this brief survey.

Translator's note: Both theology and metaphysics are referred to by the common term *al-'ilāhiyyāt* (literally 'theology'). Whenever theology proper only is meant, the phrase *bil-ma'nā al-akhaṣṣ* (literally 'in its special sense') is added. Metaphysics, which deals with general problems, is termed *al-umūr al-'āmmah* (literally 'the general issues').

8. Translator's note: Some of these reasons are as follows: (1) Every human being is aware that his daily acts, such as going to the market or having a walk, depend on his will; he is free to do them if he likes and to abstain if he so chooses. (2) If all our acts were imposed upon us, there would be no difference between a virtuous act and a wicked one; whereas it is obvious that even a child can distinguish between a kind and a cruel act and will enjoy the first and detest the second. If all our acts were determined by God, they would be all alike; that is, there would be no difference between good and evil, between virtue and vice. (3) If God creates all our acts, it is pointless for Him to command some things and forbid others and consequently to reward and punish accordingly. (4) If we are not free in our acts, it is unjust of God to create sins in creatures and then punish them on account of sinning.

9. Translator's note: The notion of motion in leaps (*ṭafrah*) was first suggested by al- Naẓẓām. It means that a body undergoes discrete leaps during motion. The modern parallel of this idea of motion is one employed by quantum mechanics. In 1900 Max Planck put forward the hypothesis that the charged particle – usually called the oscillator or vibrator – that is the source of monochromatic light absorbs and emits energy only in discrete quanta. It changes its energy not continuously, as was supposed in the classical

theory of radiation, but by sudden jumps (*ṭafrah*). In 1913 Niels Bohr, applying quantum theory to subatomic phenomena, published the quantum theory of the atom. Since then quantum mechanics has become an important part of atomic physics.

10. Translator's note: The verses 57:22 and 4:78 seem to convey a meaning contradictory to that of 4:79 and 18:29. While the former imply total predestination, the latter explicitly support the idea of freedom. The Ash'arites attach basic importance to the former and the Mu'tazilites to the latter kind. The Shī'ites reconcile the two sets of verses and take an intermediary position. The following traditions from al-Shaykh al-Ṣadūq's *al-Tawḥīd*, 360–62 (Jamā'at al-Mudarrisīn fī al-Ḥawzat al-'Ilmiyyah, Qum), explain the *shī'ī* position:

Al-Imām al-Bāqir and al-Imām al-Ṣādiq (A.S.) said, 'Indeed God is of greater mercy than that He should coerce His creatures into sin and then punish them for that; and God is of greater might than that He should will something and it should fail to happen.' They were asked, 'Is there any third position between absolute predestination (*jabr*) and absolute freedom (*qadar*)?' They said, 'Yes, vaster than the space between the heaven and the earth.'

... Muḥammad ibn 'Ajun says, 'I asked Abū 'Abdillāh (A.S.), "Has God left men free [to do what they may like]?" He replied, "God is nobler than that He should leave it up to them [to do whatever they may like]." I said, "Then God has imposed their deeds upon them?" He said, "God is more just than that He should coerce a creature into committing some act and then punish him on its account."'

... Ḥasan ibn 'Alī al-Washshā' says, 'I asked al-Imām al-

Riḍā (A.S.) whether God has given men total freedom in their acts. He said, "God is mightier than that." I said, "Then, has He coerced them into sins?" He replied, "God is more just and wiser than that He should do such a thing." Then he added, "God, the Almighty, has said, 'O son of Adam! I deserve more credit in your virtues than yourself, and you deserve more discredit for your sins than I; you commit sins with the power I have given you.'"'

... Al-Mufaḍḍal ibn 'Umar reports that al-Imām Abū 'Abdillāh (al-Ṣādiq) (A.S.) said, 'Neither total predetermination (*jabr*), nor total freedom (*tafwīḍ*), but a position intermediate between the two (*amr bayna amrayn*).' I said, 'What is *amr bayna amrayn*?' He replied, 'It is as if you see someone committing a sin. You stop him, but he does not desist. So you leave him alone. Then if he commits that sin, it does not mean that since he did not heed you and you left him alone, you asked him to commit it.'"

See also Murtaḍā Muṭahharī, *Insān wa sarnewisht* ('Man and Destiny'), for an elaborate discussion of this point.

11. Translator's note: Some historians have advanced the theory of a connection between Mu'tazilite theology and the 'Abbāsid movement. H. S. Nyberg, in his article on the Mu'tazilites in the *Shorter Encyclopedia of Islam*, after remarking that 'Wāṣil adopted a somewhat ambiguous attitude regarding 'Uthmān and his murderers and that he left undecided the question of knowing who had the superior claim to caliphate, Abū Bakr, 'Umar, or 'Alī,' says that, 'All these apparently dissimilar lines converge on a common centre: the 'Abbāsid movement. It is precisely Wāṣil's attitude which we must regard as characteristic of the partisans of the 'Abbāsids . . . Everything leads us to

believe that the theology of Wāṣil and the early Mu'tazilites represents the official theology of the 'Abbāsid movement. This gives us an unforced explanation of the fact that it was the official doctrine of the 'Abbāsid court for at least a century. It seems even probable that Wāṣil and his disciples took part in the 'Abbāsid propaganda . . .' Although Nyberg's conjecture is not sufficient to establish this hypothesis, further research may bring to light some conclusive evidence in the matter.

12. Translator's note: Akhbārism is a movement that started within the *shī'ī* world about four hundred years ago. Its originator was Mullā Muḥammad Amīn ibn Muḥammad Sharīf al- Astarābādī (d. 1033/1623–24). He openly attacked the Shī'ites *mujtahidūn* in his work *al-Fawā'id al-Madaniyyah*, vehemently contesting the Uṣūliyyūn's claim that reason is one of the sources of *fiqh*. The Uṣūliyyūn hold the *Qur'an*, the Sunnah, reason and *ijmā'* (consensus) to be valid sources for deduction of the rules of the *sharī'ah*. The Akhbārīs accepted the validity only of the Sunnah and rejected the rest. Understanding the *Qur'an*, they claimed, is beyond the capacity of an ordinary person, being restricted exclusively to the Ahl al-Bayt (A.S.).
Regarding *ijmā'*, they said that it was an innovation (*bid'ah*) of the Ahl al-Sunnah.
Reason, they held, is valid only in empirical sciences. Its applicability cannot be extended to the realm of the *sharī'ah*. Accordingly, they rejected *ijtihād*, considering the *taqlīd* (following the authority, imitation in legal matters) of a non-*ma'ṣūm* as forbidden. However, they considered the reliability of all the *aḥādīth* of the four books, viz. *al-Kāfī*, *al-*

*Tahdhīb*, *al-Istibṣār*, and *Man lā Yaḥḍuruhu al-Faqīh* as being authentic and undisputable. They held that it was the duty of the people to refer directly to the *ḥadīth* texts in order to discover the commands of the *sharī'ah*. There was no need of the *mujtahid* as an intermediary. The Uṣūliyyūn, in particular such scholars as Āqā Muḥammad Bāqir al-Bihbihānī (1118/1706–1205/1788) and Shaykh Murtaḍā al-Anṣārī (d. 1281/1865–66) refuted the Akhbārī position and effectively repulsed the threat posed by them to the *shī'ī* institution of *ijtihād*. Some prominent Akhbāris among *shī'ī* scholars were Sayyid Ni'mat Allah al-Jazā'irī (d.1050/1640), Muḥammad ibn Murtaḍā Mullā Muḥsin Fayḍ al-Kāshānī (d 1091/1680), Shaykh Yusuf ibn Aḥmad al-Baḥrānī al-Ḥā'irī (1107/1695–1186/1772), and Ṣadr al-Dīn Muḥammad ibn Muḥammad Bāqir al-Ḥamadānī (d. after 1151/1738–39)

13. This treatise has been published as an appendix to his *al-Lum'ah*, and 'Abd al-Raḥmān al-Badawī has included it in the first volume of al-*Madhāhib al-Islāmiyyīn*, 15–26.
14. See, Muḥammad Abū Zuhrah, *Ibn Taymiyyah.*
15. Murtaḍā Muṭahharī, *Āshnā'ī bi 'Ulūm-e Islāmī* ('An Introduction to the Islamic Sciences'), see the section on philosophy, the fourth lecture entitled 'Rawish-haye Fikrī-ye Islāmī'.
16. The Qur'an, (2:285).
17. This is the stand on *ṣifat* that is usually attributed to the Mu'tazilites. Ḥājī Sabzawārī (in *Manẓūmah*, his philosophical poem) says:
    al-Ash'arī bizdiyādin qā'ilah
    wa qāla binniyābati'l Mu'tazilah

However some Mu'tazilites, such as al-Hudhayl, have held a position exactly similar to the *shī'ī* position.

18. Murtaḍā Muṭahharī, *'Adl-e Ilāhī* (Divine Justice).
19. Ibid, the discussion on *shafā'ah.*

# Index


**A**

'Abbāsid, 5
'Abdulāh ibn Aḥmad Abū al-Qāsim al-Balkhī, 37
'Abdullāh ibn 'Umar, 35
Abāḍiyyah, 13
Abū 'Alī al-Jubba'ī, 37
Abū al-Ḥasan al-Khaiyyāṭ, 37
Abū al-Hāshim al-Jubba'ī, 37
Abū al-Hudhayl al-'Allāf, 50
Abū Bakr, 31, 44, 68
Abū Ḥanīfah Nu'mān ibn Thābit, 15
Abū Ḥātam al-Rāzī, 14
Abū Isḥāq al-Isfarā'yinī, 40
Abū Ja'far al-'Iskāfī, 37
Abū Ja'far al-Aḥwal, 50
Abū Ya'qūb al-Sijistānī, 14,15
*'adl*, 16, 53, 54, 55, 57, 58
*aḥādīth*, 8, 38, 69
*aḥkām*, 1
Ahl al-Ḥadīth, 10, 12, 13, 28, 37, 38, 39, 40, 47
Ahl al-Sunnah, 12, 18, 28, 37, 38, 39, 41, 42, 43, 45, 46, 69
Ahl al-Tawḥīd, 20
Aḥmad ibn Ḥanbal, 12, 37, 39, 40
*akhlāq*, XI, 1, 2
*A'lām al-Nubuwwah*, 14
*al-amr bil ma'ruf wa al-nahy 'an al-munkar*, 2
*al-Asfār*, 61
*al-aṣlaḥ*, 42
*al-Bayān wa al-Tabyīn*, 36
al-Ghazālī, 40, 41, 44
al-Ḥasan al-Baṣrī, 3, 26, 34
al-Imām al-Hādī, 51
al-Imām al-Jawād, 51
'Alī ibn Ismā'īl ibn Maytham

al-Tammār, 50
*al-i'tizāl*, 34
al-Ka'bī, 37
*Al-Kāfī*, 50
*al-kalām al-lafẓī*, 43
*al-kalām al-nafsī*, 43
al-Ma'mūn, 36, 37, 40, 45, 51
*al-Mawāqif wa al- Maqāṣid*, 38,41
Al-Mufaḍḍal, 68
al-Mu'taṣim, 36, 45
Al-Mutawakkil, 37, 45
al-Qāḍī 'Abd al-Jabbār al-Astarābādī, 17
al-Sayyid al-Murtaḍā 'Alam al-Hudā, 17, 40
*al-taklīf bimā lā yuṭāq*, 29
*al-tawḥīd al-'ibādī*, 18, 19, 20, 56
*al-tawḥīd al-af'ālī*, 18, 20, 21, 22, 56, 57
*al-tawḥīd al-dhātī*, 18, 19, 20, 56
*al-tawḥīd al-ṣifātī*, 18,19, 20, 21, 29, 34, 56,57
*al-Uṣūl al-khamsah*, 17
*al-wa'd wa al-wa'īd*, 16, 24, 35, 53
al-Wāthiq, 36, 37, 45
al-Zamakhsharī, 37
Amīr al-Mu'minīn 'Alī, 4, 23, 44, 45, 46, 47
'Amr ibn Abī al-Hudhayl al-'Allāf, 25, 47, 49, 50, 51
'Amr ibn 'Ubayd,27,35, 46,50
Ash'arites, 4, 10, 18, 20, 21, 22, 23, 24, 31, 37, 40, 41, 45, 48, 56, 57, 58, 59, 60, 62, 63, 67
*'aqā'id*, 1, 2
*aṣl al-tanzīh*, 34
*'ayn al-yaqīn*, 62

**B**

*badā'*, 61
Banū al-'Abbās, 36
Banū Umayyah, 33, 36
Bāṭinīs, 13, 14
Battle of al-Jamal, 35
*bid'ah*, 12, 70
*bisāṭah*, 48
*burhānī*, 48

**C**

Christians, 5, 38, 65

**D**

*Da'ā'im al-Islam*, 15
Dār al-Taqrīb Bayna al-

Madhāhib al-'Islāmiyyah, 14
deanthropomorphism, 42
Divine Acts, 6, 23, 29, 34, 43, 60, 61

F

Faḍl ibn Abī Sahl ibn al-Nawbakht, 51
Faḍl ibn Shādhān al-Nīshābūrī, 51
*fāsiq*, 13, 16, 25, 27, 30, 33, 35, 43, 47, 63
free will (*ikhtiyār*), 3

G

Ghaylān ibn Muslim al-Dimashqī, 3

H

*ḥajj*, 2
Ḥamīd al-Dīn al-Kirmānī, 15
Ḥamrān ibn A'yan, 50
Ḥanafī, 10, 14
Ḥanbalī, 10, 14, 20, 40, 48
Ḥasan ibn Mūsā al-Nawbakht, 52
*ḥikmat al-'ishrāq*, 48
*ḥikmat al-mashshā'*, 48
Hishām ibn al-Ḥakam, 50
Hishām ibn Sālim, 50
Holy Prophet (S), 4, 55
*ḥudūd*, 17
*ḥudūth*, 10, 48
*ḥujjah*, 56
*ḥusn*, 23, 34, 42

I

Ibn al-'Amīd, 45
Ibn Qibah al-Rāzī, 52
Ibn Taymiyyah, 12, 20, 40, 70
Ibrāhīm ibn Sayyār al-Naẓẓām, 35
*Iḥyā' 'Ulūm al-Dīn*, 40
*Ijtihād*, 11,70,71
*ikhtiyār*, 3, 4, 6
*ilāhiyyāt bi al-ma'nā al-akhaṣṣ*, 29
*'ilm al-akhlāq*, 2
*'ilm al-fiqh*, 2
*'Ilm al-kalām, 1*
*'ilm al-tawḥīd wa al-ṣifāt*, 2
*'ilm al-yaqīn*, 62
Imām al-Ḥaramayn al-Juwaynī, 40, 44
Imām Fakhr al-Dīn al-Rāzī, 41, 44
Imāmiyyah Shī'ā, 14
*īmān*, 25

*Intikhāb al-Aṣlaḥ*, 60
*'irfān*, XI, 6, 41, 44
Isḥāq ibn Abī Sahl ibn al-Nawbakht, 51
Ismā'īlī, 14
*'Iṣmah*, 63
*istiṭā'ah*, 30
*istiṭā'ah qabl al-fi'l*, 42

J

*jabr*, 3, 4, 6, 58, 67, 68
*jabr wa ikhtiyār*, 33
Jabriyyah(Jabrite),3,4
*jadalī*, 48
Ja'farī, 10
Jahm ibn Ṣafwān, 34, 47
Jalāl al-Dīn al-Suyūṭī, 13
*Jāmi' al-ḥikmatayn*, 14
Jews, 5, 38
*jihād*, 2

K

*kabā'ir*, 25
*kāfir*, 16, 24, 25, 26, 27, 30, 43, 63
*Kashf al-maḥjūb*, 14
*kathrah*, 48
Khawārij, 13, 14, 25, 26, 27, 28, 31, 33, 35, 43, 47, 63
*khulf al-wa'd*, 25
*Khuwān al-'Ikwān*, 14
*Kitāb wajh al-Dīn*, 14
*kufr*, 13, 24, 25, 33, 36, 47

L

*luṭf*, 42

M

*ma'ād*, 7, 53, 54
Ma'bad al-Juhanī, 3, 33, 47
*mabda'*,7
*Maghfirah*, 63
Magians, 5, 38
*makhlūq*, 10, 36
Mālik ibn Anas, 13, 39
Mālikī, 10, 14
Mānawiyyah (Manichaeans), 65

*Manzilah bayna al-manzilatayn*, 16, 26, 35, 43, 47, 53, 63
*Maqālāt al-Islāmiyyīn*, 43
Ma'ṣūmūn, 60
Māturīdiyyah, 65
Mawlānā Muḥammad al-Rūmī, 44
Mazdakiyyah, 64
*miḥnah*, 10, 37, 40
*milal wa niḥal*, 34

*mi'rāj*, 62
*mu'min*, 16, 30, 43
*Mu'aṭṭilah*, 64
*muḥaddithūn*, 38, 49
Muḥammad ibn 'Abd al-Wahhāb, 20
*mujtahid*, 11, 70
*mujtahidūn*, 11, 38, 69
*mukallaf*, 29
Mullā Hādī Sabzawārī, 53
Mullā Ṣadrā, 52
Mu'min al-Ṭāq, 50
Murji'ah, 10, 13, 26, 31
*mutakallimīn*, 4, 5, 7, 17, 18, 29, 32, 33, 41, 49, 51, 52, 53, 60, 64
Mu'tazilites(Mu'tazilah),, 4, 10, 12, 15, 16, 17, 18, 20, 21, 22, 23, 24, 26, 28, 30, 31, 32, 33, 34, 35, 36, 37, 38, 39, 40, 41, 42, 43, 44, 45, 48, 53, 56, 57, 58, 59, 60, 61, 63, 67, 68, 70

N

*nafy al-tashb*īh, 34
*Nahj al-Balāghah*, XII, 25, 48, 64
Nāṣir Khusraw al-'Alawī, 14
Nawbakht, 51
Nīshābūr, 51

P

prophethood, 1, 4, 8, 54, 55

Q

*qabīḥ*, 24, 25
*qaḍā' wa qadar*, 6
*qadar*, 33, 67
*qadariyyah*, 3, 4, 33, 34

Qāḍī Abū Bakr al-Bāqillānī, 40
Qays ibn Māṣir, 50
*qidam*, 10, 29, 48
*qubḥ*, 23, 34, 42,59

R

*Risālah fī Istiḥsān al-Khawḍ fī 'Ilm al-Kalām*, 40
*Ru'yah*, 61

S

Sabaeans, 5, 38
Sa'd ibn Abī Waqqāṣ, 35
Ṣāḥib ibn 'Abbād, 17, 37
*ṣalāt*, 2
*ṣawm*, 2
*Sayrī dar Nahj al-Balāghah*,

48,65
Seljūq, 45
Shāfi'ī, 10, 14
Shī'ites, 10, 13, 18, 46, 48, 49, 52, 56, 57, 58, 61, 62, 63, 67, 69
Ṣiffīn, 25, 35
*Ṣiḥāḥ*, 46
*ṣirāṭ*, 46
*ṣūfis*, 62

T

*ṭafrah*, 30, 66
*tafwīḍ*, 58, 68
*Ṭaḥāwiyyah*, 66
*Tahdhīb al-'Akhlāq wa Taṭhīr al-A'rāq*, 52
*taḥkīm*, 25
*Tajrīd al-I'tiqād*, 52
*Tajrīd al-I'tizāl*, 41
*tanzīh muṭlaq*, 42
*taqwā*, 1
*tarkīb*, 48
*tawbah*, 16
*Tawḥīd*, 16, 18, 19, 56, 67
temporality, 10, 48

U

*umūr 'āmmah*, 28
*uṣūl al-Dīn*, 1, 2, 8, 53, 54
*Uṣūl-e Falsafah wa Rawishe Ri'ālism*, 13, 48,66
Uṣūliyyūn, 38, 70,71

W

*waḥdah*, 48
Wāṣil ibn 'Aṭā', 31, 47

Z

Ẓāhiriyyah, 66
*Zanādiqah*, 5, 65
Zayd ibn Thābit, 35
Zaydī, 10
Zaydiyyah, 14
*zindīq*, 65
*ẓulm*, 22

www.ingramcontent.com/pod-product-compliance
Lightning Source LLC
Chambersburg PA
CBHW021446080526
44588CB00009B/717
*9781922583185*